AND THAT'S THAT!

The Life Story of One of Golf's Greatest Champions

———————————

Louise Suggs

With Elaine Scott

authorHOUSE®

AuthorHouse™ LLC
1663 Liberty Drive
Bloomington, IN 47403
www.authorhouse.com
Phone: 1-800-839-8640

Front Jacket Photo: Associated Press

Editor: Gerald McClanahan

Published by AuthorHouse 06/12/2014

ISBN: 978-1-4969-1413-2 (sc)
ISBN: 978-1-4969-1412-5 (hc)
ISBN: 978-1-4969-1414-9 (e)

Library of Congress Control Number: 2014909333

This book is printed on acid-free paper.

Contents

To Mom and Dad
Marguerite and Johnny Suggs
They started it all

Foreword

George and I have been privileged to travel the world, attend grand balls, meet artists, athletes, not to mention countless heads of state, but it is the friendships we have made along the way that we cherish the most. Louise Suggs led the charge for women's professional sports organizations and is one of the amazing athletes to which we formed a lasting friendship.

I first met Louise on Sea Island, a place that George and I hold dear to our hearts. We enjoyed our honeymoon there, and returned over the years to celebrate various anniversaries. It was the occasion of our 46th in 1991 when George "gave" Louise to me as a gift. I had a lesson with her, and then we went to play a few holes with a couple of friends. I striped my first drive 230 yards—maybe only 130 yards—regardless, I couldn't contain my excitement. I grabbed Louise's arm, raised it in the air and declared, "That's what a lesson with Louise Suggs will do for you." Not only did this woman dominate the women's tour for so many years, she was also a terrific golf teacher.

In honest, humorous, "Louise style," *AND THAT'S THAT!* divulges Louise's early years discovering the game of golf and her favorite memories of life along the way. I truly admire her courage and zeal for life and have loved my friendship with her.

Barbara Bush
First Lady of the United States, 1988-1993

Preface

ODE TO GOLF

I wonder sometimes what it's worth to me
These hours I spend on the practice tee?
And then I conclude that it's quite all right
To be slashing away from morning till night
If you love the old game as much as I
There can be no limit except the sky

—*Louise Suggs*

I tell you, it's been a trip—a life that I wouldn't change for the world. And that's that!

As we went through the process of deciding what we wanted to call this book, Cari Gardner, a dear friend who is really much like a daughter, reminded me that, more often than not, when I finish telling one of my stories I will say, "And That's That!" She was convinced it would be a perfect title for the book. As I stewed on it longer, her point made perfect sense. I suppose I had got into the habit of saying, "And That's That," because I've always considered my stories to be a simple point of fact—just part of living a life. But, as the years went by, so many folks that I love and respect kept encouraging me to put my life's reflections and stories into a book.

So here it is, my life story! I was so grateful to work on this book with my friend, and another one of my "kids," Elaine Scott. We talked for untold hours, pulling these many memories out and putting them on paper. I met Elaine over 25 years ago when she was just a young pup working in the communications department at the

LPGA. I knew, because of how we connected over the years, that she was the one I could trust to bring life and truth to my stories.

Throughout my whole life, I have deeply appreciated the acknowledgement of what I've been able to accomplish in the game. It has seemed even more so in recent times, as I've been recognized in various ways for what I did all those years ago—so much so, it has led me to joke that I'm more famous now than when I was famous!

I feel very fortunate to have had a talent, one that I was able to use to build a career. But it doesn't make me any different than some guy down the street. It has always amazed me how when some people play a sport well or they do something that gets their name or picture in the paper, they immediately change personalities. They think, "I'm better than that son of gun over there and I'll show them," and they somehow create a world around themselves that's fake. Well, I can't be anything except what I am—and if you don't like it, lump it.

It's been a blessed life in so many ways, one for which I'm very grateful. I look back on my career; the tournaments I won, the many special people I met, the places I've been, and the things I never could have experienced if I hadn't played this great game. When I do that, I remember that someone at Lithia Springs, where I grew up playing golf, said, "You'll never make a golfer, why don't you do something else?" I thought to myself, "By God I'll show you." And I think I did.

As I said in my dedication, it all started with my beloved Mom and Dad, Marguerite and Johnny Suggs. Beyond them, there have been so many other people who have enriched my life along the way.

My golfing hero, the incomparable Bobby Jones, ignited my love of golf and inspired my career more than I could ever put into words. My golfing mentor, Dot Kirby, was the greatest role model I could have had.

My Aunt Vera and my younger brother, Rell, were an important part of my very happy childhood. My late fiancé Mac didn't return from the War, and so we didn't start the family we'd planned. But, as life went on, I have always had a dear and intimate circle of friends who I consider to be my true family. Among those, my lifelong friend and companion Jean Hopkins brought great wisdom and humor. And, I grew a bunch of "kids" in Cari Gardner and her three boys (Steve, Chris, and Jason), Elaine Scott, Cindy Davis, and Ty Votaw. They are very dear to me, and I tell them often not to forget that I taught them everything they know!

I don't know what I'd have done without the wonderful and unconditional friendship of Nancy Lierle, Pat and Cartan Clarke, Cathy Levering, and Susan and Andy Quinn.

My extended LPGA family also will always be special: Commissioners Charlie Mechem and Mike Whan; former communications head Connie Wilson; Marlene Hagge—one of my running buddies from the LPGA's Founding days; and players Beth Daniel, Meg Mallon, and Karrie Webb. They too should never forget that I taught them everything they know!

At Sea Island and Ocean Forest, my deepest appreciation to Bill and Sally Jones, Judy and Claude Booker, Ann Heins, Charlesetta Cross, Sue Sayer, Frankie Strother, and the rest of the terrific staff who always make me feel so welcome.

Other friends who always help so much: Stephanie Fender, Barry Rubin, Molly and Kevin Dorval, Fred Devitt, Thomas Smith, and Peter Nicholson. And, not forgetting back in my beloved Georgia, some folks who really encouraged me to write this book and helped get some of the facts straight from my early days in the game: Wayne Aaron, Gleda James, Betty Rich, John McGoogan, and Mike Waldron. And, I share Elaine Scott's deep appreciation for our editor, Gerald McClanahan, and his boundless patience and wisdom.

So, this is my life story. Ninety years in the making. It's been a heck of a ride. Good, bad and indifferent—it's one I would do all over again. And that's that!

Louise Suggs

It All Started with a Great Fire

For Johnny and Marguerite Suggs, four o'clock in the morning on Friday, September 7, 1923, represented the happiest moment of their young married life. It was the birth of their first child, Mae Louise Suggs. As they basked in the radiance of this eight-pound-five ounce bundle of joy, little did they know that just hours later that spark would be usurped by a great blaze—to be more accurate, an historic fire that glowed over Ponce De Leon Avenue and lit up the northeast side of Atlanta, Georgia. To this day, for many in Atlanta, September 7 is remembered as the anniversary of a fast and unforgiving inferno that completely destroyed the spectator stands at Spiller Field, home of their beloved baseball team, the Atlanta Crackers. But, in the world of golf, that date in 1923 is important for something completely different—it is the moment one of the greatest players to grace the grand old game had been born. And, for anyone lucky enough to know Louise Suggs, it's of little surprise that the first day of her remarkable trailblazing life is still marked by the memory of an historic fire.

I was born in the early hours of the morning in Wesley Memorial Hospital in Atlanta, which is now Emory University Hospital. Later that day, Dad had just gotten home from the hospital when the phone rang. It was a friend of his who said urgently, "Johnny you'd better get down to the ballpark, it's on fire." Well Dad, thinking he was being pranked by a buddy upon the birth of his first child, laughed and hung up on him. Moments later, the phone rang again. This time it was the telephone operator. You see, in those days when you picked up the phone, the operator was already on the line and would say, "number please," and would then make the call for you. She had obviously heard the previous conversation and said, "Really Mr. Suggs, believe me, you'd better get down to the ballpark. It is on fire."

Sure enough, the entire wooden structure at the ballpark was burned to the ground in just a matter of hours and with it the team's uniforms, trophies, and all the records. The ballpark was on Ponce de Leon Avenue, across the street from the iconic Sears and Roebuck building which I remember watching being built in 1926. Spiller Field, or Old Poncey as it was later known, is still chronicled as the only ballpark to have a tree in the middle of the field. A magnolia tree grew in deep center field. If a ball got hung up in the tree, it was still considered in play. In fact, Babe Ruth became one of only two players to hit an in-park home run right into it. Now the park is gone, but that century old tree, which survived the 1923 fire, still remains after all these decades with a plaque at its base—a symbol of the grand old days of southern baseball when the Crackers became the all-time winningest team in the old Southern Association. My maternal grandfather, Rell J. Spiller, owned The Atlanta Crackers baseball team and Spiller Field, and my father worked for him at the time.

Grandfather, a successful man who rose from being a grocery clerk to become a wealthy concessionaire, entrepreneur, and sports enthusiast, worked with Dad to completely rebuild a stadium out of the ashes. His mission was to make it the pride of what was then the AA Southern Association and he achieved that goal by constructing the first steel and concrete park in the South. It could hold up to 20,000 fans and it became known as the most magnificent ballpark in the minor leagues. The ball team went on to flourish and was nicknamed the Yankees of the minors. Grandfather owned it from 1919 until 1932, when he sold it to The Coca Cola Company. It then continued as Atlanta's ball team until 1965 when The Braves became the city's Major League franchise.

My father came to know Grandfather before he met my mother because Dad was himself an accomplished ball player. He was originally from Lincoln, Alabama, and played ball at Auburn before enlisting in the War. After serving over in France, he returned home and was snapped up as the left-handed pitcher for the Atlanta Crackers from 1919 to 1922, and really showed his stuff in 1921 when he pitched a no-hitter against Memphis.

During the time that Dad was on the team, my mother Marguerite helped out in the concessions area. The moment Dad first set eyes on her was a particularly steamy summer day in 1922. He walked into the concessions area to see her sitting on top of the ice cream cooler trying get a chilly breeze up her skirt. He always said he took one look at her and decided in that moment, "Wow, any woman that hot, I gotta marry."

After their marriage, Dad was loaned out to the New York Yankees for a while, since they really didn't have farm teams in baseball in those days. He went to spring training in 1923 to try out with the Yankees, but the team's manager Miller Huggins told him the Yankees would only have one left-handed pitcher and a deal had been made with the Boston Red Sox for Herb Pennock. He said, "Johnny, go back to Atlanta and we'll call you up to try again next year." It was a shame, because he was so good that Babe Ruth complained he couldn't hit Dad's pitches during practice—and isn't that the point? Anyway, by that time I was on the way and it suited Dad to come back to Atlanta and just work for Grandfather running Spiller Field, rather than get traded to another team. He later said, "I was countryman enough to not like being traded around like a mule. I have never regretted it." And that turned out to be the truth.

For the Love of Family

I've said many times that I credit my family for who I am, and for what I've been able to accomplish. I had an especially happy childhood, and cannot say enough about how much I respected and admired my parents. Because we grew up during the Great Depression, things weren't always easy. But Mom and Dad never let on that life wasn't anything but normal, and my younger brother Rell and I never went without—not just in ways of sustenance, but also with encouragement and structure.

Dad was influenced by the fact that his own father and mother let him make his own decisions about his career. When he came home from Alabama Polytechnic to say he was going to enlist in the army, they supported him. Then, when he came home and wanted to play baseball, they also left that up to him to make the decision. He and my mother did the same for me. When I knew I wanted to play golf for a living, they were entirely supportive. And that was no small thing in that era when you consider that I was a girl. Dad once admitted that when Mom was pregnant with me, he was hoping for a left-handed son that he could develop into a great pitcher. Well, I was pretty ambidextrous my whole life, but I wasn't a left-handed pitcher. Dad later conceded that he wouldn't trade me for a dozen left-handed pitchers—with Lefty Grove and Carl Hubbell thrown in.

My mother was Lessie Marguerite Spiller Suggs (1903-1981). She was Dad's right-hand man, so to speak, and without doubt the power behind the throne. She didn't much care for the limelight, and was perfectly happy to let Dad and me be the ones out front. She just kept us out of trouble as best she could.

Mom was a very talented woman—an accomplished pianist with a lovely soprano voice. Frankly, she was quite the prim and

4

proper type—kind of a debutante you might say. As an only child, she wasn't allowed to have any pets and she would have nothing to do with athletics. She never even picked up a golf club, always saying that someone had to keep some sanity in the family. I always knew how proud of me she was but she couldn't understand why I was outside hitting golf balls rather than sitting inside playing with a doll.

I have her to thank for grooming me with the manners and etiquette that have helped me so much throughout my life. To this day, Mom's words still come to mind when it comes to using the right knife and fork at a formal dinner. She was a real lady and I'd like to say that it rubbed off on me. I was always immaculately dressed for every occasion. When I went out of the house, she made sure I was clean and neat and had my hair combed, particularly if I was going into town. Even though I have always been an athlete, I was kind of prissy when it came to my appearance and I have always been a neat freak—and that's because of my mother. If Mom gave me a chore to do and I didn't do it just like she wanted, she'd make me go and do it again. Believe me, it made me learn to do it right the first time.

I knew I had graduated in her eyes to a certain degree when I was about 14 or 15 and said, "Mom, may I please have a Coke?" She looked at me and she said, "You know, I think you're old enough to know when you can have a coke and I know you won't abuse it. Just whenever you want one, go and get it." Well, I thought, "Wow, I'm grown. I've arrived." It's strange, but that moment has always stood out to me as an important time in my life.

When she married Dad she got into a whole new way of living. When Mom met Dad she was a student at North Avenue Presbyterian School in Atlanta, a prep school for Mount Vernon Junior College in Washington D.C. As such, she ended up not going to college. Despite that, they had a very equal relationship and really complemented one another. He was a rough sportsman who loved to hunt and fish.

Mom loved the trophies, but said that she hated having to clean them.
Photo copyright 1940-1949, Estate of Bessie Walker Callaway.
All rights reserved. Used with permission.

I used to hunt quail with him and fish. In fact, I could bait my own hook—take fish off the hook and all that kind of stuff. But Mom didn't like any of that. Wouldn't do any of it.

When it came to my competitive golf career, I always thought that how I did in a tournament didn't mean all that much to her. But, as time went on, she would call the newspaper to see how I was doing. She called the paper so much that it finally got to the point where whoever was on the phone at that time of night would recognize her voice and say, "Oh, Mrs. Suggs, the scores haven't come in yet." She wouldn't let on with me, but she just had to know.

■ ■ ■

My father was John Braden Suggs (1896-1979). A World War I veteran, he played baseball in college and then joined the pro leagues when he came back from the War. When he met Mom he was pitching for the Crackers, the Atlanta team owned by my maternal grandfather. He took up golf while he was still playing for the team and got to where he could shoot in the 80's and, eventually, 70's. He claimed that all pitchers have rabbit ears trained to hear remarks, both laudatory and derogatory, from the grandstands. So, when golf professionals came around, he would eagerly listen to the information they gave out in return for baseball chitchat. He always said that the transition from baseball to golf was painless.

Dad was a good man. He was very emotionally expressive and a funny guy to boot. You never knew what he was going to say. I've always believed that he had more influence on me as a person than as a golfer, even though he was the one who taught me the most of what I knew about the game.

His lessons didn't only come on the golf course. For example, during the war there wasn't any gas to drive anywhere or balls to play golf. So, for something to do we'd play pool together, a nickel a game, and I got to be a pretty good player. That later came in good stead with my putting because one time he said to me, "If you see a putt that's on a break, how do you figure it?" I got to thinking about it and realized it was sort of like pool. How you bank it off and angle the shot. He said, "You got it kid."

Now, Dad really didn't make me get into golf. In fact, at one point, he tried to convince me that golf was for men. Well, when you tell a kid, especially me, not to do something, you'd better know that I would break my neck to do it. If he had coaxed me into playing golf, I'd probably have decided to play football. It was reverse psychology in a way.

Dad once locked up my clubs for two months after he saw me wrapping a club around a pine tree. It really taught me a lesson.

Believe me, I didn't throw any more clubs after that and eventually became quite even-tempered.

As I became more established in the game and really began contending in tournaments, Dad would get more nervous than I would. Ma Keeler, wife of the legendary sports writer O.B. Keeler and a friend of our family, was quite the character herself. One time, in her Southern twang, she said, "Johnny, now if you're gonna watch the young 'un, don't you let her see you and get all excited and not think about her golf game." Well, he tried so hard to keep out of sight that in one tournament I ended up getting more distracted by watching him hopping from behind one tree to another. Finally, I caught up to him and said, "Dad, get out where I can see you. Just walk around. You're making me more nervous."

There was another tournament where I had won one of my matches on the way to the final. Afterward, he seemed so uptight while we were sitting and having a coke. I reached over and touched him and found that he was as hard as the table. I said, "Are you cold?" And he said, "No, I'm just so nervous." He was almost shaking. I ended up winning that tournament and I swear I thought he was going to break my ribs when he grabbed me and hugged me so hard.

■ ■ ■

"My sister is a genius." Rell Suggs, quoted by George Trevor in the New York Sun

My brother Rell Jackson Suggs (1925-1993) was two years younger than me. He was in the Navy during the war and afterward went to Georgia Tech. He later transferred to Auburn, where he played on the varsity golf team. Eventually, I helped get him a job at MacGregor where he became a territory rep in Oklahoma, Arkansas, Louisiana, and Mississippi.

Rell and I were fairly close growing up. Everything went pretty well between us as long as I could beat him up. But when he got to where he could beat me up, things got a little rough.

Rell was also a pretty good golfer, and once caddied for me in an LPGA tournament in Oklahoma, which was part of his MacGregor territory. At that time, that tournament took place in the fall and, as such, all the caddies were in school. Instead, the event organizers used the civic clubs' members as caddies. Knowing that Rell was my brother they thought it would be great if he caddied for me. Little did they know it was the worst thing they could have done. If I wanted to use a certain club and he didn't agree, when I tried to take it out of the bag he'd hold it so that I couldn't get it out. Why we didn't get in a fistfight I don't know.

■ ■ ■

While Mom was an only child, Dad had one brother, Sanford Eugene Suggs, and one sister, Vera Suggs. Aunt Vera was an artist who lived in Miami. I always enjoyed being around her since she was interested in different things besides golf. I'd have to say she was a great influence on me for many reasons, especially because I liked art. I would fool around with it and sometimes got in trouble as a result. I didn't quite paint the walls, but I came close. I have often thought that if I hadn't followed the golf path I might have made a decent architect.

On one occasion when I was about 12 or 13, I was visiting Aunt Vera in Miami and she caught me messing around with her paints, which was a complete no-no. So instead of punishment she took me into town and bought me what you might call a beginners art kit. She set me up, showed me what to do, and had me copy a picture out of a magazine. Well, I did it to the best of my ability. While it wasn't anything that put me on the map as an artist, I was quite proud of

Rell and me at Spiller Field in 1929.

it. I'm sure Aunt Vera was thinking, "This kid had better stick to golf." I always kept that painting. Almost 80 years later, the original piece of artwork is still on display at Cherokee Town and Country Club in Atlanta.

The End of Baseball and the Beginning of Golf

Lithia Springs is the site of an ancient natural mineral water springs, believed to be over 5,000 years old. It still functions today. The water is naturally full of lithium, potassium, calcium, and other rare earth elements and trace minerals that for centuries have been considered to be a healthful elixir. Local folklore says that before burning Atlanta in the Civil War, General Sherman sent a detachment of his Union troops to the springs to fetch him some of the water. As years went by, the area became so known as a center of wellbeing that crowds came and sometimes even camped on weekends to enjoy the proclaimed healing powers of the water. In taking notice of this, businessmen took to capitalize on the popularity and began bottling the water and, in 1888, built a health resort—the 250-room Sweetwater Park Hotel. A Lithia Springs Railroad ran between Atlanta and Lithia, bringing all kinds of celebrities and dignitaries to the area for a dose of health. Lithia water, often prescribed by doctors for its health attributes, continued to be distributed all over the country into the 1920's. Unfortunately, the hotel burned to the ground in 1912 and was never rebuilt.

It was the early 30's when Grandfather sold the Atlanta Crackers and the baseball field. Around that time, like so many, The Depression got the better of him and he lost most of the wealth he'd accumulated over the years. He had, though, previously bought and still owned a piece of property in Austell, 20 miles west of Atlanta. While today Austell is considered a suburb of Atlanta, back then it really was in the country. What Grandfather owned was Lithia Springs and, hence, a new chapter of my life began around the site of another devastating fire.

When Grandfather moved all of us to Lithia Springs, he and Dad restarted the bottling business under the name Fountain of Youth

Bottling Company—the Lithia Springs Water Co., and Grandfather distributed the water until he died in 1946. He produced the SPAX brand of Lemon-Lime-Lithia carbonated water. The springs are still in use today, with bottled products produced and marketed under the Lithia brand name. Looking back, when I was a kid none of us ever really got sick. I suppose it makes sense, come to think about it, that it was the water.

It was at that time that Dad began building the Lithia Springs Golf Course—the place where my golf career was seeded. Even though Dad was a farm boy, his parents found a way to send all three of their children to college. Dad was in the class of 1919 at Auburn. He studied what, in those days, was called Animal Husbandry but now would be landscape engineering. Because of that, he knew all about drainage and built a nine-hole course all by himself with just a mule and a drag pan. He did all the work except for what little help he could get out of five teenaged boys he hired from time to time. With the property naturally littered with granite boulders, he designed the course around the rocks and kept them in place as natural obstacles. One particular boulder behind the fifth tee became the icon of the course. It is still there today. We called it Frog Rock—obviously, because it looks like a frog. When the media began to show an interest in my golf, there were numerous times we did photo shoots with me posing on Frog Rock.

After all of Dad's backbreaking work, Lithia Springs Golf Course opened in 1933, right at the height of The Depression. It wasn't a long course—about 6,000 yards. It had two par-5s; one was about 495 yards and the other was close to 520. It cost 25 cents to play nine holes and 50 cents for 18 during the week. On the weekends it was 75 cents and a caddie would set you back a quarter per nine. When he went up to a dollar, everyone gave Dad fits. All of that said, it was reasonably successful and it made us a decent living and a good way of life.

Frog Rock became an icon on the course at Lithia Springs. It remains there today. Photo copyright 1940-1949, Estate of Bessie Walker Callaway. All rights reserved. Used with permission.

In those early days, there weren't any power mowers at Lithia Springs, which meant that the fairways were cut by a mower drawn by our mule, Jack. Dad took care of the greens himself with a hand mower. I really don't know how he did it but I'm sure his strength from being an athlete must have helped him. I had my own job on the course too. Every day I had to fill the sandboxes and the water pails. Beyond that, I would follow Dad around the course, a golf club in hand, and as he finished each green I would drop an assortment of all kinds of misshapen golf balls on the grass, hit them up, and putt out. We would repeat that routine hole after hole until Dad had cut every green. Looking back, I suppose that's where my good short game came from. Dad had a real green thumb and became well known as one of the South's authorities on course maintenance. Those greens were as smooth as anything. Later in my career, I always said that if I could have taken those greens around with me I would have won a lot more titles.

There wasn't much that Dad wasn't capable of doing to make sure the course was in great running shape. For example, we had a bunch of ladies who regularly played and they kept complaining that there wasn't a toilet on the golf course. Well, because we were in the country, we couldn't have any running water so Dad built a fancy two-holer and put a toilet seat on it over by the seventh hole. It was the best spot on the course because it was as far away from the clubhouse as you could get. Going in there wasn't without its dangers. Wasps, yellow jackets, and other things would build nests in there, so the key was making a lot of racket to find out if anything was in there before going in. The alternative, going in the bushes, always seemed more desirable to me.

In addition to the course, Dad also built houses at Lithia for our family. Ours was right by the first tee and our grandparents' was close by on a hill. It was a great place to be as a kid and I'd have to say altogether it was a really happy childhood. As time went by, Dad decided that Lithia Springs needed a clubhouse, so he converted the building where they originally had bottled the Lithia Water. It was a huge building and Dad fixed it so that a quarter of the building featured a dance floor and he put in a jukebox. On Friday nights, since there wasn't anything else to do, all the kids in town were invited to the clubhouse. They'd ride their bikes over and Dad would trip the jukebox so we could all dance. It was a great thing for all of us because the kids got to have fun and the parents didn't have to worry because they knew where their kids were.

It came to Mom to take care of the pro shop and the club restaurant. She made all the visitors and members feel welcome, and did the planning for the numerous parties we had for various groups of people. We had a cook named Travis and I could always tell we were going to have a party because I'd hear Mom yell, "Travis, go and shave." I can still hear her. She ran that restaurant like she really knew what she was doing. If folks came in to the golf club restaurant needing service, she would get up and take care of them. When the two of us kids became old enough, it was our turn to take care of customers—even if we were eating dinner, which was just fine. We did it.

Because of Grandfather losing his money in The Depression, I guess you could say we were poor but nobody really knew it. In my mind, we were never without because we had each other.

Grandfather, who I always remember wearing a straw hat, had been very entrepreneurial. He had some pretty wild ideas. For example, he had alligator wrestling at one time at the ballpark. I've always thought that it was that side of him that attracted my

Grandfather Spiller, Mom, and our dog, Nancy.
Photo copyright 1940-1949, Estate of Bessie Walker Callaway.

grandmother, Clara Mae Pound Spiller. I really admired her. She was a person before her time. In fact, she was the first woman I ever saw in pants. She wore plus fours to go walking and hiking around Atlanta, when even Atlanta was considered rural and country.

I remember vividly how tough Grandfather could be. My parents had to ask for money when they needed it and they didn't have a car, which meant that they also had to ask when they wanted to go anywhere. One time when I got going in competitive golf, Grandfather told me that if I didn't play representing Lithia Springs he wouldn't feed me. Luckily, because Dad always had a healthy perspective and a good sense of humor, he was able to just deal with it. And, thankfully, he really loved my mother so it was all worth it to him in the end.

A Great Place to Grow Up

Despite Grandfather's toughness, thanks to Mom and Dad we really had a fun time growing up. My brother Rell and I would get a quarter on Saturday nights and we'd ride our bikes into the small town of Austell to a little café. We could get a coke and a hamburger for a dime. Then we'd go to the movie where we'd get admission and a bag of popcorn for 15 cents. We were never without anything to do.

There was an area in town where all of us kids had been begging for a tennis court. Eventually Dr. Ragsdale, the owner of the property, said we were allowed to have it if we built it ourselves. And that's exactly what we did. It was red clay and, I must say, we did a pretty good job—even painting the lines on our own. At that time, I was quite a good tennis player. I was always pretty agile and could get around the court well. However, it came to the point where Dad said, "You have to make up your mind, tennis or golf." It wasn't a hard choice for me. Because even though I was good at tennis, I was much better at golf.

When I consider kids today, I always think it's a shame that they can't get out and about with the same kind of freedom as we did in those days. We were really good at being self-entertained. Grandmother wanted me to be a piano player, but I always thought, "Why would I be inside practicing when I could be outside playing football?" It was much easier to get dirty than it was to practice on the piano. I was always outside getting dirty, either running, jumping, riding a horse, and swimming because we were fortunate enough to have a pool at Lithia. But, much like tennis, swimming eventually had to go once I got more and more serious about golf and realized the stroke is completely different from the golf stroke. It trains a different set of muscles. I was pretty good at basketball too, but one day I jammed my fingers and realized that wasn't going to be good for my golf either, so that came to an end. Photography became something I really enjoyed. I would take photos with a big folding camera. I had a lens fast enough to stop golf swings and would often take photos of people on the course and had pictures pinned all over my bedroom. I would build model airplanes and, at one point, I really thought I'd like to learn to fly. But, I didn't want it to get in the way of my golf and it became another thing I had to let go. No complaints though, and no regrets as I look at how my career unfolded.

Dad with Rell (age 12) and me (age 14) as we practice putting at Lithia Springs.

■ ■ ■

When you live in the country, you don't have access to city water and sewage. Dad had to build his own well and Gould pump.

The minute you turn the tap in your house, it starts the pump and it brings water out of the well. He got a well-digger to dig the well, which was probably 30 feet deep, and then had it lined with cement drainage pipes. Each year he would scrub it down after pumping all the water out of it. However, the pump wouldn't get the last couple of feet of water and it wasn't big enough for a man to get down, but it was, unfortunately, big enough for me. So that meant down a thin ladder in a bathing suit I went to help bucket out the remaining water. Once all the water was out, I'd yell, "Dad that's it," and he'd say, "Okay," and surprise me by pouring a bucket of ice-cold water over me. Every year he did it and got a good laugh out of it. And every year he caught me by surprise. The last time he did it I said to him, "I'm never going to tell you it's the last bucket again." He chuckled and said he was surprised I hadn't said it sooner. He had that kind of humor. What a joker he was.

■   ■   ■

With that kind of life, there were lots of things folks would do for each other to get by. One day, soon after the course was opened, a guy in his early 30s drove up, came in to the club, and introduced himself as Dr. Frank Clark. He said, "I've just got my license and have come to set up a new medical practice. Mr. Suggs, somebody told me that possibly you could help me out. The only thing I own is that Model A Ford out there and 25 cents in my pocket. If you could help me out, if you could feed me until I get on my feet, I guarantee you'll have medical treatment from me for you and your family and you'll never have to pay a dime for it." Dad agreed and Dr. Clark was true to his word. He took care of Mom and Dad as long as they lived in Austell. Their friendship became so close that when Dr. Clark was going to get married to his wife Margaret, he asked Dad to go with him to help with the drive and be his best man in Fargo, North Dakota. After the ceremony, they just got in the car and started driving back south. The first night, they stopped in a hotel and that's when things got a bit awkward. Dad had to go from his room and through theirs to go to the bathroom. What an interesting honeymoon night that made! Needless to say, it became a long-standing joke between them.

Later Dr. Clark gave me the putter that I used through my entire amateur career. In those days, when you bought a set of clubs, no matter what, a putter came with it. When Dr. Clark bought a new set for himself, he didn't want the putter because he still liked the one he already had. The one he gave me was a Walter Hagen with a steel spiral shaft. It was a trusted friend of mine, that's for sure. It is now displayed in the United States Golf Association museum.

■   ■   ■

School, which was in Austell, was another part of childhood I really enjoyed. To get to there, I would walk each day down Spring Street, which was just dirt then. Most of my classmates were farm children and they would ride the bus to school. We had to be at school at quarter of eight, had just 20 minutes for lunch, and got out at 1:15 pm. The reason for that timeframe was so the kids could get back and have time to help out on the farm. It makes sense now, looking back, that our school uniforms were overalls.

We were the War babies, and most of the boys wound up in service. My homeroom teacher one year was Miss Louisa Cloud. My goodness she was a scary person. She had a long narrow face with a fierce expression, and looked like a ghost. Although I later came to know her as a very nice person, all she had to do was look at me and it made me want to duck under the desk.

I was a good student. If I was given a job to do, I did it. At the study hall, most kids cut up and played, but I studied. I knew that if I got my lesson done for the next day I wouldn't need to take that book home. So a lot of times I'd go home and Mom would say, "Where are your books?" And I'd say, "I already did all my lessons."

We had a class project in geography one time when I was in the sixth grade. The task was to build something and explain what it was. So, I found an old piece of pinkish colored marble and a box, and made the marble fit the box. I made a road and a mountain and a little house. I took it to class and proudly announced to my teacher, "This is my project and this is where I may go on vacation some time." I was just being silly, but she said, "You did that yourself?" She was so impressed she had it displayed in the front hall. As a kid, when you see that kind of reaction and you get recognized with credit for doing something, it makes you imagine that you are capable of doing other things too.

There were 25 kids in our class—13 boys and 12 girls—and I graduated Valedictorian on May 31, 1940 at the age of 16 and had to make the first speech of my life. That was just two weeks before I won my first Georgia State Amateur Championship. At age 15, my report card read: Spelling 97; History 95; English 95; French 96; Chemistry 95; Days present 175; Days absent 5; Times tardy 0. The five days absent were for the 1939 Georgia State Championship.

I remember when I was 16, I wanted to play in the Georgia State High School tournament, but we didn't have a golf team or anything. Despite that, the superintendent of the high school, Mr. Howard, found out what he had to do to enter me. He drove me up to Athens, Georgia, and I played in the tournament as one of only two girls. The other was Mary Winkenwerder, who was from Waycross, Georgia, and was the same age as me. I won the little gold medal and she won the silver. Good old Mr. Howard. He didn't know a golf ball from a football, but he gave me the opportunity to do that. When we got back to school, he really spouted off about it, telling everyone all about it during assembly one morning.

■ ■ ■

Gleda James, a local historian, former mayor of Austell, and owner of today's Lithia water company, successfully lobbied the city of Austell for five years to buy the remaining 50 acres of the old golf course and name it the Louise Suggs Memorial Park. Her vision included engraving one of the original granite boulders in honor of Louise. Under the watchful eye of the iconic Frog Rock, Louise and numerous golf industry dignitaries were present in September 2010 for the official groundbreaking for the park, a joint venture between the city and Douglas County. Gleda remains an energetic and inspired advocate of keeping Louise's remarkable life and accomplishments prevalent, not only in Austell, but also statewide. She has organized numerous local school field trips to the old course site to educate them on its storied history.

Getting in the Game

There is no doubt that I got my innate competitive spirit from Dad. I really believe it's something you either have or you don't. It's not necessarily something someone can teach you but Dad surely knew how to bring it out in me. He was always saying, "Bet ya you can't do so and so," which just fired me up to where I'd say, "Bet ya I can!" And then I'd do it. It worked every time. As a youngster, I had no concept of having athletic talents but I clearly inherited those genes from Dad as well. So, whether it was running, jumping, any kind of ball game, or even marbles, I could beat almost anybody. Because we were in the country, I didn't have many play friends. The kids I hung with were usually the caddies, who were also my schoolmates from the local farms. They were all boys, because back then young women wouldn't even have been thought of as caddies.

Now, there were always plenty of things for us to do as kids, and many that I would have been good at, but because my backyard was a golf course I began to fool around with the game at the age of ten. Seeing that I was beginning to show an interest, Dad fixed me up with a mishmash of sawn-off clubs; a set that was given to him for hitting the only home run of his career. In those days, Spalding had a promotion with the Southern Baseball Association where they'd give a set of clubs to any pitcher hitting a home run. In his case, he got a set of wooden-shafted A.G. Spalding and Brothers. Dad cut those clubs down to length for me and wrapped bicycle tape around the grips. I guaran-darn-tee you, with that kind of tape on your hands, there was no way you could turn that grip loose—even if you wanted to. So, that's how it began.

As golf went from being just something to do to a sport that I really began to get serious about, I have no doubt that one of the things that brought out the best in me and helped me become a better golfer was a game I played with the boys called Short Knocker. In essence, we'd all hit the ball and the one who hit it the shortest was, of course, the Short Knocker. That person then had to go and pick up all the balls. And then we'd do it all over again. Obviously no one wanted to be the Short Knocker, especially me, so it taught me to just hit the heck out of it. That's probably how I learned to hit the ball so long. I wasn't longer than all the boys, but I can tell you that I was never the Short Knocker. I suppose you could say it also helped develop my competitive spirit.

There were a bunch of other games we would invent that began to shape my swing. For example, the caddies and I had an area where we played that was all dirt and no grass. We'd make holes in the ground with various obstacles and the object, obviously, was to get the ball in the hole. That forced us to get creative and maneuver the ball to make it do the right thing. I also remember a day when I was bored and standing on the cement patio of the clubhouse. It seemed like a fun idea to get my 9-iron and start hitting shots off the concrete. Well, if you don't want to jam your hands and ruin your club, you learn in a hurry to hit the ball first. And, cleanly at that. These were the kinds of things that I really credit with helping me use my imagination in the development of my shot-making skills.

Want to focus on accuracy and really know your target? How about hitting drives and having someone catch them for you in a baseball mitt. That's exactly what I did in practice thanks to a deal Dad set up for me with my brother Rell. He'd shag for me a lot of the time and Dad said to him, "I'll give you a dime for every ball you catch, and you give me nickel for every ball you miss." Well, it got to the point where Rell was making more money than Dad could afford. So that stopped. The reason I believe I became so accurate was because I was always aiming for him. He even caught my drives. You know how a mitt will have a baseball impression? Well, his glove had a golf ball impression instead. At the time, it didn't occur to me that he could have shared that money with me. I suppose I was just glad I didn't have to pick up the balls myself. When he wasn't around or just wouldn't do it, I had to pick up my own balls. So that's when I learned that if I put my shag bag out there, aimed for it and was accurate, I didn't have to go all over the place to pick up my balls.

My putting also blossomed because Dad's greens were as good as any you would find. That stood in my favor as I learned a pretty good putting stroke and became more and more confident that I could make putts. There wasn't much grain in his greens, which was amazing since Lithia was just a cow pasture when he got it. But he knew how to grow grass and he made sure he was always learning. He'd go to other courses in Atlanta and pick their brains. He told me once, "When you get up on a green, or before you get on the green, look at the undulation. Figure out as best you can which way the green tilts, because that's the way the water is going to run off it; whether it's hand watered or rain watered. If there's any grain in the green, it's going to go with the flow of the water."

So things progressed pretty fast for me. By the age of ten, I could shoot in the low 50's around Lithia's nine holes. Three years later I was shooting in the low 80's over 18. That's when I got my first pair of golf shoes. Until then, I either played in tennis shoes or sometimes in bare feet. If I had been riding in the morning, helping Mrs. Beldon exercise her horses, I would have my riding boots on. In that case, I'd play golf in the afternoon in my riding boots.

Then one day, when I was 14, a chance encounter changed everything and put me on a whole new track. Mom and Dad had never really talked with me about getting competitive in golf, but this particular day was about to shift everything. Martha Daniel, the reigning state champion of Georgia, happened to be driving on her way somewhere when she came past our course. She stopped

All the days of practice at Lithia Springs paid off.

off and decided to play nine holes by herself. I didn't see her at first because I was out hitting balls. And even if I had, I didn't know who she was. I was still practicing when she finished playing and went into the clubhouse. It so happened that Mom and Dad were in there and she said to them, "Who is that kid out there?" They looked up and said, "She's ours." Martha said, "Well she can really hit a golf ball, did you know that?" To that, Dad said, "Yeah, I guess I've seen it." In his defense, there was nothing to compare me to in those days. No other women golfers, kids, junior golf—anything like that. So Martha said, "I think the girl can really play golf. The Georgia State Championship is a month away at Druid Hills in Atlanta. Why don't you enter her and see what happens?" And so Dad called Ma and O.B. Keeler, who he had known from his ball club days. O.B.

was a sportswriter for the *Atlanta Journal* who became legendary by following the career of Bobby Jones and chronicling his every major tournament win, and O.B.'s wife, Ma, always travelled with him. Ma said, "Sure, I think the young'un will do alright."

So there it was. At the age of 14 I went off to my first-ever tournament. Here's where it got interesting—until that day I'd never seen a bunker in my life. Dad didn't put any traps in at Lithia Springs. He did that so that play would keep moving along. I suppose that's when it dawned on me—I really didn't know much about golf. I didn't have a club more lofted than a 7-iron, so you can imagine how it went for me when I got in my first bunker. Not well. I finally came to my wits and decided that the best way to get out of the sand was to hit the ball out backwards and then play back up to the green. Most kids would have just gotten mad and kept trying to come out the front. I suppose that's what you call manufacturing a shot. The whole experience left me in tears that first night.

Sixteen players got through the stroke play qualifying round to the match play part of the championship, and I was the last one to qualify with a 92. I lost my first match and then I lost my match in the consolation round to Caroline Dykes. I will never forget her. She was from Columbus, Georgia, and was probably 18 years old at that point. To me, she was my senior and so I kept saying, "Yes ma'am" and "No ma'am" until she finally she turned on me and said, "If you call me ma'am one more time, I'm going to hit you." No more needed to be said after that.

After the consolation round, they had a pitch and putt contest where they set up three tees of different lengths from one cup on the 18th green. We hit three balls from the three tee-off spots. Much to everyone's surprise, I shot a six with a two on each ball. That was unheard of, so they said, and I got a silver plate. I still have it at home somewhere. I was so proud of that plate. It was the first thing I ever won playing golf. When I got home I went down to the jewelry store and had my name engraved on it. My name was almost bigger than the plate.

I think back on that experience and I know that I looked around and thought to myself, "I like this." And that's when I realized that I had a real taste for competitive golf.

When we got back to Lithia, Dad built me a sand box and he put it right behind one of the granite boulders that were all over the course. That thing was about seven or eight feet high, and he put it back about only five or ten yards beyond the trap. He said, "Now, get over it." Believe me when I say, if you didn't get over it and the ball hit that granite boulder, you had to be ready to duck. Still, a 7-iron is all I had and I learned to flip that ball over the boulder. For the rest of my career (and afterward) I could get out of a bunker almost better with a 7-iron than with a wedge.

I proved my point later on when I lived in Delray Beach, Florida. I belonged to a club called Pine Tree Golf Club. We had quite a group of members—Beth Daniel, JoAnne Carner, Meg Mallon, and Karrie Webb. We all happened to be out on the practice tee one time, just joking around, and for the fun of it I clocked off and said, "I bet you a buck I can get closer with a 7-iron out of that practice bunker than you can with a wedge." Well naturally, they jumped all over me like fleas on a hound dog. Being a senior, they gave me the honor, and I hit one up there to about 18 inches. Nobody, got inside of it, and they used wedges. They all wanted to have another go, but I said, "No, just one time," and I took their money and left. I often wondered if they ever went back out to try it with a 7-iron to see if they could do it.

There really is only one way to do it—you use your hands and wrists to flip it and make sure that the blade is square. Most think you need to open up the face, but if you do that with a 7-iron you're going to shank it every time. Just take the club outside, be sure that your weight is more or less on your left foot, even though you're behind the ball, and then just flip it. The magic is really in your hands.

The year following her first appearance in the Georgia State Women's Championship, Louise came back to the tournament; this time at Glen Arven Country Club in Thomasville, Georgia. In an interesting stroke of irony, in the semi-final she met the very person that had ignited her desire to play competitive golf, Martha Daniels. Louise handily disposed of the tournament favorite by 5 & 4. Colleen Butler, in turn, beat Louise in the final to leave the fifteen-year-old with the runner-up salver in just her second showing at the state level. However, at the featherweight of just 100 pounds, Louise created the biggest stir of the week by winning a driving distance award for the championship division with an impressive average of 236 yards.

O.B. Keeler noted Louise's runner-up finish and went on to point out that Bob Jones once won a driving contest at the St. Louis Country Club, in a field of entries for the U.S. Amateur Championship, with an average of 228 yards. "The turf was pretty wet and heavy," Keeler wrote, "but still—well, you see the point."

Despite winning that driving contest, I'd have to say my most vivid memory of that year's championship came on the 11th hole. It was an uphill par-5 called "Long Tom." Well, I hooked a ball, heard it rattling around, and assumed it was in the trees. When I got there, instead of it being in the trees, I discovered that I'd actually hit my ball inside a maintenance building. My ball was in the middle of a long barn with a door on either end. It had come to rest under a huge mowing machine. Fortunately, there were some caddies following the match and they rolled that mower out of the shed for me. We then opened the door facing the green, I took a 2-iron, and I just hit it straight out of the barn. I remember thinking to myself later, "That was kind of dumb, but I got away with it," and I did get a half on the hole. Of course, in those days we were playing matches instead of medals so you could go for those kinds of things. I suppose I reminded myself that I would pretty much have a go at anything.

During those first few years, I can't really tell you that I realized I was talented. I was a big hitter but wild and all over the place. One time I was playing in a tournament and Ma Keeler was there. She heard a ball hit into the trees and bang around, and she said, "That's got to be the young un' in the pine trees," and she was right. I could knock the heck out the ball but I never knew where it was going.

Because of my two Georgia State appearances, I was beginning to get noticed but my folks weren't necessarily pushing me to play in a bunch of tournaments. It was difficult for them because I couldn't drive and they had to take me if I was playing away from home. However, in the winter after I turned 16 it was decided that it would be okay if I went down to Miami to stay with Dad's sister, Aunt Vera, and play in the 1940 Miami Biltmore Invitational in Coral Gables. When I was staying with Aunt Vera, I rode the bus to the course each day with my golf clubs and my shoes hanging off the bag. I even had to transfer buses en route. I didn't realize, and nobody told me at first, that I could leave my bag at the club. So, of course, here I come, walking in to the Biltmore with my clubs on my shoulder and some snooty folks starting making some wisecracks. It rattled me and left me in tears. I realized later that they liked picking on me because I was from the South and had a drawl. It was there when I met Helen Hicks for the first time. She walked in on one of the teasing sessions and said, "Leave this kid alone. You'd better be careful because she is going to beat you out there on the golf course one day." From that moment on, I was attached to her like adhesive tape. I always looked up to her. She was one of the first women in golf to turn professional.

Eventually, I found my own voice and could stick up for myself. All the kids on the amateur circuit were mostly Yankees and they'd tease me about being a Rebel and how we got beaten. One time, they were all doing it at the Orange Blossom Hotel in Orlando. I finally banged my hand on the table and said, "Well they didn't beat me!"

Me at age 16—the year I began to travel and play in more tournaments.

It was at the 1940 Miami Biltmore Invitational that Louise really began to turn heads. She won her first match and then in the second round met Patty Berg; five years her senior and the dominant player in amateur circles with three Titleholders Championships and a U.S. Amateur title. Patty had also been the winner of the Biltmore event the previous three years. Both players started out strong. After five holes, Louise was three up and was outdriving Patty on some holes. However, word started getting around about what was going on and people were rushing out to watch. Louise lost her composure and Patty regained the lead after nine. Eventually, Patty prevailed with a 4 & 3 victory, but was later compelled to say, "Her name isn't Louise. It's Dynamite for me. I was just lucky to be going at

31

top speed. You know the old saying, the score doesn't tell the story." Even Patty's father, Herman, said that Louise had perhaps the finest swing with a driver in the whole field.

After my match, I watched every hole I could with these great players. I felt like they had something I didn't, especially around the greens where they could get their short iron shots to sit down like a poached egg. I decided in that moment I would never stop trying and went back to Lithia to keep working on chipping and putting.

Morgan Blake, columnist for the Atlanta Journal *wrote a poem for the paper after Louise's match against Patty:*

A WARNING TO PATTY
I trust you will not think me catty,
If I suggest that Mistress Patty
Has really too much on the ball
For those gal golfers—one and all;
When that red-head gets good and hot,
It's just too bad for Betty, Dot,
For Ellamae and Shirley Ann,
And others of the female clan;
So rule the roost, Pat, while you may,
For Louise Suggs is on the way;
I'm thinking in a year or two
Louise will put the skids on you.

His words quickly began to ring true when, a month later, Louise beat Marion Miley by 4 & 2 in the final to win the 1940 Augusta Invitational at Forest Hills in Augusta, Georgia.

Louise graduated from high school at the end of May and because her grade point average was so high, she didn't have to take finals. Instead, she prepared to play in her third Georgia State Championship, just two weeks later, at Columbus Country Club. This time she came away as champion at the age of just 16. Johnny Suggs was watching, in O.B. Keeler's words, by "snooping from tree to tree, unable to talk to anyone."

And that was it. One of the greatest amateur careers in the history of golf was already on its way to the history books. There was no looking back.

The Career before the Career

Even after I won the Georgia State Championship in 1940, it really didn't cross my mind that I could make a career out of golf. I was studying Latin and French in high school with the hopes of going to Emory University later that spring. However, in those days, finances were tough for my folks and they could only afford to send either Rell or me to college—but not both. It went without saying that in those days they sent the boy. Instead, I ended up getting a job right after I graduated from high school.

There was a man called Bill Reid who played at Lithia Springs and was a friend of Dad's. He happened to work for Gulf Oil Corporation in Atlanta and somehow he and another colleague got the bright idea that they needed a file clerk in the Gulf Oil office. In hindsight, I know they were just trying to help a kid like me get a break. Before I had time to think about it, they had hired me for $25 a week and I began making the daily drive from Austell into Atlanta to work in the Hurt Building.

I worked straight through to the following spring of 1941 before I took my first vacation. That's when I went to Memphis to play in the Women's Southern Amateur. Well, I won it and, without much hoopla, dutifully turned up back at work the following Monday. When I got back to my desk there was a note—"See Mr. Etzel." Walter Etzel was an assistant division manager of Gulf and, to be honest, I thought I was going to get fired. I'd never met the man— didn't even know where the heck his office was so, in my mind, for what other reason would he want to see me? I finally found his secretary who took me in to meet him. Now I didn't know that he was partially deaf, which made him grumpy. He looked up, saw me, and growled, "What do you want?" Here I am, just 17 years old, and I replied, "You sent for me," and I went on to explain who I was. He said, "You won that golf tournament?" To which I replied, "Yes, sir." "Well, from now on you're working for me," he said. After that, I quickly learned that this guy was a real golf nut. He had been transferred from Gulf Oil's home office in Pittsburgh. Nobody liked him in the Atlanta office because he was a "damn Yankee" with different ideas and was more progressive than his laid-back Southern co-workers. Well, who was I to argue with him? So I said, "Yes, sir." He gave me a company car and an expense account. He instructed me, "If I want you to do anything, you are to stop what you're doing and come do what I tell you to. Is that clear?" To which I once again said, "Yes, sir."

Suited up for work at Gulf Corporation in downtown Atlanta.
It was a fairly small town back then, and I walked all over calling on customers.

They put me in the service station department. Because gas stations were about service in those days, my responsibility was to monitor the dozen or so company stations in town where I would make sure that the restrooms were clean and the guys working there were in clean uniforms. On top of that, I had to make sure the commission forms were filled out every month for those guys in our commission stations or they wouldn't be paid. When the War started, all the guys went into service and Gulf started hiring women. I ended up in charge of these women. I never had any problems, but a couple of them were pretty tough and, being as young as I was, there were times I was scared to death.

As time went on, Mr. Etzel called me in and told me that the company was starting a new program and they wanted me to be part of it. They introduced a Gulf Oil credit card that was offered to newcomers who brought businesses to the greater Atlanta area—folks that our credit manager, Arch Haley, deemed to have a good credit rating. The card could be used for any product or service at any of our Gulf stations. It was up to me to take the cards when they were issued and contact these people. I would go to their place of business to personally welcome them to Atlanta, offer and explain the point of cards, ask if there was anything Gulf could do for them, and invite them to play golf. If they wanted to play, the company had memberships at Eastlake and Capital City Club. In many ways, I was really acting as a Gulf Oil ambassador for folks moving to the South.

When I look back on it, if it hadn't been for Walter Etzel I wouldn't be where I am today. Through my job, he gave me the opportunity to regularly practice and play golf on some great courses and he became somewhat of a father figure to me. It got to the point where I'd say, "Mr Etzel, can I play golf this afternoon?" and he'd say, "Don't ask me. Just tell me where you'll be." And that was how our relationship worked. Years later, a friend of mine,

Joe Lee, a golf course designer who worked under the world-renowned designer Dick Wilson, ran into Walter somewhere and got to chatting. Walter said, "Louise did more for our company at that time than anybody else." Of course, Gulf never told me that. But it was nice to hear.

The Going Gets Serious

"No other golfer—not even Bobby Jones or Ben Hogan—ever held so many important titles at one time or exerted so strong a dominance in his field."—Ed Miles, Atlanta Journal

Louise Suggs won 14 nationally prominent amateur titles in eight years, going unbeaten in over 60 matches in the most important tournaments in the game. She won every amateur event in which she was eligible to compete, sometimes more than once—and that's despite the fact she missed three seasons of events during her peak amateur years because of the war. When she turned professional in 1948, Louise was the reigning champion in: the Southern Amateur, the North & South, the Western Amateur, Western Open, U.S. Amateur, and the British Ladies Championship. Some called it Louise's own grand slam.

From left: U.S. Women's Amateur, Women's Western Amateur, Women's Western Open, and Women's Southern Amateur. Photo courtesy USGA.

My professional career is a source of great satisfaction for me. However, I'd have to say that I'm proudest of my amateur record. I always had a feeling that when I played against somebody I was going to win, if it was the last thing I did. I didn't lose many amateur matches and I guess it was because I was such a competitor. Wanting to win was a natural instinct. In hindsight, I was probably one of the best match play players to ever come down the pipe—if I do say so myself. You just don't win that many matches in that caliber of tournaments in the same year. You might win one or two, but you're not going to win five or six.

It's obvious that I was born with a competitive spirit and applied it to everything I did. Marbles, dominoes, relay races, swimming, diving, pretty much anything—I was ready. I guess I was just built that way. It was never for adoration or fame—I just wanted to win. Simple as that. When we started playing for money in the early LPGA tournaments, there was one event where, if I had two-putted on the last hole, I would have broken the record. The 18th had a tricky undulating green and I was winning the tournament by several shots. I knew if I three-putted I'd win the tournament and if I tried to make the first putt for the record and I missed, I might four-putt. It was that kind of green. So I thought to myself, "I'll just three putt it," and that's what I did. Afterward, I got jumped all over by a couple of people who said, "Why didn't you go for the record?" I said, "I won the tournament, didn't I?" I wasn't interested in breaking records because records don't stand. I held the record for a long time for lowest score at the U.S. Women's Open, but ultimately it didn't last. The number of wins never goes away, and winning is what I wanted. It just came naturally to me.

Louise's first significant win had come at the age of 16 in the 1940 Georgia State Championship. A year later, at the age of 17, she won the nationally renowned season opening Championship of Champions tournament in Punta Gorda, Florida, by 3&2 over Betty Hicks. Louise had

10 one putts on the way to victory and later learned that Betty had been pegged to walk away with the title.

The 1940 Georgia State Championship.

Louise's national prominence rose rapidly later that spring when she won the Southern Amateur—beating Texas star Peg Chandler 7&6 in the 36-hole final. After 10 holes in the morning, Louise was eight up but went into lunch four up. That victory ignited media and nationwide chatter about this rising star just about the time Louise was preparing to play in her first U.S. National Championship at Brookline in September. Louise turned 18 the week of the event.

I was excited and nervous all at the same time about playing in the National Championship. What a tremendous experience. The only disappointing moment of the whole event was the unfortunate run-in we had with Joe Dey, who was the executive director of the USGA at the time. Even though I had been given honorary memberships at both Eastlake Golf Club and Capital City Club in the summer of 1941 after I won the state championship, my grandfather and I had filled out my application to play in the National Championship by listing my home course as Lithia Springs. After all, that is where I lived and learned to play. Well, unbeknownst to us, the USGA did not recognize nine-hole courses and they denied my application and sent back our check. When we realized this, we completed a new application listing my membership as Capital City Club.

Unfortunately, when I arrived at Brookline and went out for my first practice round, Joe came out and gave me all kinds of grief about finagling a membership from Capital City just to get into the Championship. Of course it wasn't true, but he just wouldn't leave it alone and pretty much reduced me to tears. It was almost as if he was saying I wasn't good enough to be one of them. For a while after that, Joe kept questioning my amateur standing because I was working for Gulf Oil in various administrative capacities through my amateur career. I finally gave him a paycheck stub to prove that I was actually doing real work for them. As time went by, things got better and Joe and I became pretty good friends.

In 1942, the North & South Championship at Pinehurst was the next oldest amateur tournament after the U.S. National Championship. Louise ended up victorious in the final against local icon and North & South dominator, Estelle Lawson Page. All square coming to the 17th, Louise made jaws drop with a booming drive and second shot that put her over the back of the 454-yard, par-5 hole. Veteran Pinehurst fans were amazed. They had never seen a woman hit shots of that distance. Louise birdied the hole to go dormie and then halved the 18th with a par three to win the championship. Page, who was known to win just about everything in the Carolinas, had won the event five times—including the three previous years. She, in fact, went on to win the following two years after Louise's surprise victory against her.

Estelle didn't hit it that far, at least not as far as me, but around the greens she gave me a lesson. Before 1942, she had beaten me every time I played her. My caddie's name was Butler and when he wasn't caddying he was a preacher. For some reason he didn't like Estelle at all, so when I won he just grabbed me and hugged me. Well, being that it was 1942 and we were in the South, I'm pretty sure the gallery just gasped to see me let a black guy hug me like that. It didn't bother me one bit. He'd worked hard all week and had been a great help.

Three months later, Louise won her second Georgia State Amateur Championship, continuing the solidification of her record as a force with which to be reckoned. It was clear that this golfing phenom was the real deal—proving to be nearly unbeatable in the women's amateur ranks right up until the day she turned professional.

■   ■   ■

World War II forced a three-year hiatus in amateur golf tournaments. Louise continued to work for Gulf Oil during those years, joining the ranks of many other women who stepped in to day-to-day jobs while most of the nation's men were in service.

Not too many people know that during the war, in 1943, I met the love of my life and was engaged to marry him in September of 1946. It's not something I've talked about a lot because it was, for many years, a source of great sadness. His name was Howard Clifton McCracken. We all called him Mac, but his mother called him Howard. And so, of course in front of her, I did too.

Mac was an Army Air Force pilot who was first stationed in Peking (which is now Beijing) and then in Calcutta. He was flying The Hump—a military cargo route over the Himalayas between India and China. He piloted a DC4, the hot sister to the DC3, which was the workhorse of the air force in those days.

Mac and I met completely by accident. In fact, we met by literally banging heads during a rainstorm. I was playing golf at the Bobby

Jones Golf Course in Atlanta with a couple of Gulf Oil customers. It was the summer and we all got caught in one of those sudden afternoon thunderstorms and ran to one of the shelters scattered around the course. Now, these shelters were built in such a way that the sides came down and you had to duck under to get in. I ducked under one side and, to my surprise, Mac ducked under the other at the same time. The result? We hit heads and I fell down on my butt. Needless to say, he was horrified that he'd knocked me down and kept apologizing profusely. I remember that he was in uniform but had taken off his dress shirt to play in his skivvies. When the storm was over, he went his way and we went ours and I didn't think anything else about it. One of the guys in my group joked, "What, where you trying to kill that young man?"

Howard "Mac" Clifton McCracken

After our round, as I was getting ready to leave, I went to the pro shop. Billy Wilson, one of the pros said, "Louise, I have a young flyer here and he needs to go back downtown. Are you going that way?" I said yes and came to find out that it was the same guy—Mac. We found ourselves lost in conversation during the entire car ride and that was it—the beginning of a beautiful friendship. I remember poking fun at him as he got out of the car because his wool uniform pants were beginning to shrink from having been so rain soaked. I yelled some wisecrack at him like, "You'd better get yourself another pair of pants."

When I got home that night, after dropping him off at his hotel, Mom was cooking. She asked, "How was your day?" To her shock I replied, "Fine. I just met the man I'm going to marry." I told her about the encounter and she said, "Well, if you do end up marrying him, it'll make for a good story." My head was sore for days after that but I didn't mind. It was, in a way, a nice reminder of him. All of these years later, I still chuckle at the thought that I met the one man I wanted to spend my life with by butting heads!

Mac was blue-eyed with sandy colored hair and four years older than me. He was the son of a country doctor and part of a family that was pure Southern Baptist. He used to write me from abroad saying, "I played poker with the guys last night and I won ten bucks. Please don't tell mom." His mother, Martha, was quite the family matriarch. I remember one day unpacking groceries with her, and I was just folding the empty sacks when she said, "You'll be alright." I said, "Excuse me?" She said, "Anybody who can fold a paper sack like that will be alright." It was a funny way to get off on the right foot with your future mother-in-law, but it worked for me.

Mac's father, Dr. Howard McCracken, was a successful country doctor. He had his own way of sizing me up. "I want to tell you a story," he said to me one day. "A friend of mine decided to get into the cattle business. He bought a hundred head of steer and put them

44

in the pasture. A whole year went by, and no calves showed up. He just couldn't figure it out." Before he could continue, I interrupted and said, "Why, Dr. McCracken, you've got to have cows also if you want to have calves." He looked at me and said, "You'll do." And that's when I realized he had been testing me to see if I knew much about anything—and about country life in particular.

Mac was an awful lot of fun. He was a complete golf nut. He always said, "I'll teach you to fly if you teach me to play golf." I would rib him," You've got a better chance of teaching me to fly than I've got of teaching you to play golf." I never did get around to learning to fly but really would have liked to. I could beat the heck out of him on the golf course—which he didn't like at all. He was left-handed, so I'd joke with him, "No wonder you can't win. You're on the wrong side of the ball!"

He was also a bit of a daredevil. He was a member of the Caterpillar Club—a very exclusive club that you can only join, or be invited to join, by having been forced to use a parachute to save your life. Well, Mac took this young air cadet-in-training up one day in an open cockpit plane. Mac told him to do some rolls, not realizing that he'd forgotten to fasten his own seatbelt. So, when the plane rolled Mac went out. In those days they all had to wear a parachute and that's what saved him. With that, Mac joined the Caterpillar Club and got a gold caterpillar lapel pin. To this day, I still have that pin in my safe at home.

Many years later I was in Britain on the Royal Scotsman train. There were only about 20 people on board. I walked back to the club car and noticed a man with a caterpillar pin on his lapel. Thinking I was clever, I very casually asked, "Where did you get thrown out?" At first, he looked quite insulted. I quickly realized that given the fact he had faced death before deploying his parachute, my joke might have been misplaced. However, once I explained how I knew about the Caterpillar Club (I'm sure he thought a woman would never know what it was) he warmed up and we got along famously.

At the end of his last deployment, Mac was ready to come home as he'd served his time. But one day, he didn't return from his flight. It was assumed that he crashed in the mountains. They didn't find any trace of him or his plane. It was a well-known fact that if you went down over The Hump, you didn't stand much of a chance. He disappeared in June—just two months before our wedding date.

Losing Mac was the first big tragedy of my life. It took me a long time to recover. It's funny that you go along in life and never think that those kinds of things will happen to you. When they do, it's terribly difficult to accept. In fact, his mother never got over it.

I often wonder what my life would have been like had Mac come home and we'd gotten married. He had already sent his mother and father money for a down payment on a Ford automobile. Because they were rationing cars during the war, he put his name on the list for when one became available at Baxley Georgia Ford. So this much I knew—as Mrs. Howard McCracken, I'd have been driving a Ford. I doubt if I would have played golf as a professional, even though I'm certain Mac would have encouraged it. Instead, I probably would have been a typical housewife and played in amateur tournaments. Quite frankly, I think I'd have been happy with however my life turned out.

■　■　■

After the war ended in 1945, I took a rare trip out of the Deep South to play in the Western Open in Indianapolis. When I got there, I found I was paired with Babe in the medal qualifying round. Now, I'd been hearing about Babe Zaharias my whole adult life but this was my first interaction with her. Our initial meeting came about when I saw Babe walk in to the locker room. I went up to her, introduced myself, and said that we were playing together. To that, she just shrugged and said, "So what! You want me to sign your visor?" That attitude pretty much summed up the person I came to know. As it turned out, our scores were tied that day and it was clear that didn't make her happy at all. She went on to win the event that year.

In 1946, the golf scene really began to get going again. I think I lost only one match the whole year, and that was when Peg Chandler knocked me out of the National Amateur in the first round at Southern Hills. We got to the 19th hole where she stymied me. I had practiced that shot, as we all did in those days. I tried to jump the ball and hit the edge of the cup. It didn't go in. It swung out and she beat me one up. Her husband, Dan, was a retired army officer and a West Point graduate. Like Peg, he was a friend of mine. On our 19th hole, which was right by the clubhouse, I saw Dan come out with a tumbler full of brown liquid. Well, she drank that thing down like a glass of water. I don't know what was in that glass but whatever it was it surely calmed her nerves and she went on to beat me. At that point, I joked to myself and wondered if having a hot toddy was the way to go to beat the nerves.

Despite that loss, 1946 was the year I began winning serious matches and became more and more confident. I was beyond the point where other players could scare me and I was beating people I wasn't supposed to beat. It really began mushrooming from there. That year, on my way to winning the Women's Western Open in Des Moines, I beat Babe one up in my semi-final match. I was ready for her and not intimidated one bit. I will never forget the gamesmanship of her husband George. We were all square coming to the par-3 17th hole. By the time I got on the tee, George had walked ahead to the green and made certain that when I hit he was standing directly behind the hole, smoking a cigar. He wasn't there when she hit. I think it must have inspired me because I hit the ball and I swear it was going to go into the hole. I was hoping he'd swallow his cigar and get sick. While it didn't go in the hole, karma was good to me because Babe three-putted and I won the hole with a par. There was a photo of us in the papers the next day shaking hands on the 18th after I won. You could see her trying to smile through gritted teeth. She didn't like it at all because she was on her way to a third straight title. I ruined a few streaks for her.

Keeping that momentum going, I went on to win the 36-hole final against Patty Berg, which was pegged as a mighty battle between the two of us. It was an interesting final to begin with because her caddie and my caddie were brothers. In those days we had to use a caddie from the club and the better caddies got first choice of the players. The two brothers were one and two—one took Patty and the other took me. It was almost like the boys were playing against each other.

We had an interesting moment on the 10th (the 28th of the match). As I addressed the ball, I swore I saw it move and called a penalty on myself. Patty and others insisted they hadn't seen it move, but I really felt I had to do the right thing. As it turned out, we still halved the hole and I could live with my conscience. I'll never stop believing that the right things happen to you if you do the right thing. Toward the end of the match, I was one down going into the last three holes, but I chipped in on the 16th and 17th to go to the last hole one up. On the 18th, when I hit my second shot to the par-4 green, Patty was playfully shouting at my ball, "Get on the green, get on the green," because she didn't want me chipping any more in case it went in again. As it turned out, I didn't have to chip. I won the hole and the match two up.

If you stop to think about it, it's not easy to win as many matches as I did in 1946. I tried to keep the person out of it and just play the golf course. I figured, if I played the course well, that was the best I could do. If I started thinking about my opponent, I might allow myself to think, "I'm four up," or something and not try so hard.

And that's when you begin to slip. You can't do it that way because it will bite you every time.

My match play momentum that year continued right up to the Western Amateur Championship at Cleveland Country Club in Ohio. I met Mary McMillan in the final. Mary had reached the final as a real Cinderella story as she had just beaten Babe Zaharias 3&2 the day before. I beat her 11&10 over the 36 holes on a sopping wet day. It was my largest winning margin ever in match play. Somebody said to me afterward, "Why were you so mean?" I said, "I wasn't mean, I was just playing my game." No doubt, the kid was scared to death to play me. After a while you get a reputation; you just walk on the first tee and they are afraid. I will say that Mary was extremely gracious after the match. She said to the media, "I got a beating today but gosh it sure was fun. My Irish luck just didn't hold out."

Louise partnered with Ben Hogan to win the 1946 Pro-Lady Chicago Victory National Championship on Medinah No. 3. Afterwards, Hogan said, "We won, or rather, she won. It was a best ball tournament and Louise carried us when the chips were down. That was when I first discovered she was a great player." The two went on to become friends and Hogan agreed to write the foreword to one of Louise's published instruction books, Par Golf for Women. *In it he wrote, "The swing she showed in 1946 was a beautiful thing—so smooth and rhythmic, so soundly joined together—she was bound to be a winner. If I were to single out one woman in the world today as a model for any other woman aspiring to ideal golf form, it would be Miss Suggs."*

The first time I met Ben Hogan was in 1946 when I was partnered with him as an amateur in the Pro Lady Chicago Victory National Championship. The tournament director had called Mr. Etzel, my boss at Gulf, to ask if I could play and he agreed. I later came to find out that Ben didn't like the idea of playing with a woman but, thankfully, I didn't know it at the time. When he got to the club he was still in his Army Air Corps uniform and changed once he got there. Then, off we went in the rain in the first round. Ben started out fairly civil. But that was all about to change. I was playing from the same tees as Ben and to me, on Medinah's No. 3, some of those holes looked like they were half a mile long. While we were on the same team playing our own ball, I still beat him by shooting 35 on the back nine to his 36.

I'm pretty sure some of the guys in the locker room were giving him grief about me beating him. The next morning, another rainy one, we got out on the first tee and I said, "Morning Ben," and all he did was grunt. Eventually, we got hung up on the par-3 eighth just as the sun finally came out. We were sitting on a bench and I couldn't help myself. I said, "Mr. Hogan, I don't think you're a gentleman." Shocked, he turned to me and said, "What do you mean by that?" I replied, "I made the trip up here especially to play as your partner. You're going to make all this money and now you're not even talking

Ben Hogan with me at the 1946 Pro-Lady Chicago Victory National Championship.

to me." He poked back in jest, "Oh, you mean to say we're playing for money?" To which I said, "You are, but I'm not. I'm an amateur so you get the money and I just get the money clip." That moment really broke the ice and he was so much easier to be with the rest of the tournament. As the years went by and our friendship grew, the comment about the money and the money clip remained a good joke between us.

It won't surprise anyone to know that Ben was extremely impressive to play with. Despite that first encounter he was a real gentleman. He gave the impression of being surly, but if he knew you it was quite different. He was just quiet, went about his own business, and didn't bother anybody. He once told me, "If you ever gave somebody a transfusion they'd get pneumonia. I'm told I've got ice water in my veins and you do too." He was referring to how we handled ourselves during play—our attitude and persona. We were both known as players who didn't say too much and just focused on our games.

Ed Miles, golf writer for the Atlanta Journal, *wrote: "Miss Suggs scorns showmanship as such, but her golf game is so strong and precise that it is a show in itself. Her smallness of stature has gained her designation as the feminine counterpart of Ben Hogan. Her size and build are comparable and she plays the game with the same deadly seriousness and bulldog determination."*

The late, great Furman Bisher of the Atlanta Journal-Constitution *once asked Ben Hogan how he felt about Louise being called the Hogan of women's golf. Hogan replied, "That's flattering me. Louise is a better golfer than I am. Considering her physical handicaps as a woman, the demands of the game, and her scores, I say she's a better golfer. Her swing is absolute perfection."*

■ ■ ■

In 1947, Louise really established herself as the queen of women's amateur golf by repeating her wins in both the Western Open and the Western Amateur. It was a feat never before accomplished in the long history of both tournaments. In so doing, she created her own Grand Slam: the Southern, Western Open, Western Amateur, and the U.S. Amateur. She faced and beat friend and fellow Atlantan Dorothy (Dot) Kirby in each of those finals except for the Western Amateur. No other player before her had swept all those titles in one year. When Louise turned professional the following year, the buzz in the media was that the top amateur women could return to playing the field rather than just Louise Suggs. By that time, she had won more premier women's amateur events than any other golfer.

The Western Open in 1947 was played at Capital City Club. Patty Berg and I faced off again—this time in the semi-final. It was a match that many golf writers called the greatest battle in women's golf. Of course, because it was Atlanta (and Capital City was my club), I had tremendous support from the galleries on my way to beating Patty. Unfortunately, the crowds had a really tough choice the next day in the final, because Dot Kirby and I were playing against each other. She was as much a local favorite as me so it was bittersweet in many ways.

The U.S. Amateur is really the climax of amateur golf tournaments. Fittingly, in my day, it was held at the end of the season. In 1947, it was played at Franklin Hills Country Club in Detroit and I remember it was terribly windy, terribly wet, and very cold. People were scrounging warm clothes from anyone. I don't know why but I just happened to have warm clothes with me. All I wanted to do was qualify. Because it was so windy, I was using two or three clubs more than I needed and was punching the ball to keep it in play. Under difficult conditions, golfers tend to start swinging harder and faster. If people can just control themselves (and this goes for pros too) and start swinging slower, they'll be a lot better off. That day, though, I was pretty controlled and managed to lead the qualifying and come in with a 78—which turned out to be the only score under 80. As the week went on, the weather got progressively warmer, thank goodness.

My game continued to hold up as the tension built with each match. I played a really tight semi-final match against Grace Lenczyk, who was also having a great season. We ended up as Curtis Cup teammates the following year in 1948. I led by a small margin during the entire match, but Grace was such an intense competitor that I never felt very comfortable. Going into the 185-yard 16th, I was dormie three. We were both on the green but not close to the pin. I putted first, and not well, leaving myself a six or seven-footer that, believe me, looked much longer. The pressure also got to Grace because she then ran her putt by about 10 feet. So, as I'm waiting for her to putt again, I'm thinking, "Okay, if she sinks and I miss, I'll still be dormie two." To my astonishment, she picked up her ball and conceded my putt and the match. I think she was so annoyed at missing the putt that she thought it was over. You've got to keep concentrating and thinking all the time because you can get so keyed up that it's easy to become confused and make a mistake.

The next day was the 36-hole final and, once again, Louise was playing Dot Kirby. O.B. Keeler wrote in the Atlanta Journal, *"Whichever wins, in that final bout, the erstwhile golfing capital of the world, Atlanta, and the Capital City Country Club will 'hang the blooming shields of Rome' about the corridors of a great club, won by a pair of the most gallant lady golfers that ever stepped out together in a national championship."*

I was dormie against Dot when we got to the 36th hole, which ended up being the site of the best shot I ever hit under pressure. The hole was a slightly uphill par-5 with a dogleg left from the tee. I was trying to hook the ball but I overcooked it, hooked it too much, and ended up in the rough—partially stymied by a big oak tree. My lie was also on a bit of a downslope in a little swale. I had 190 yards to the green, which was up a steep slope. At this point in a match, there was no use in safely hitting out sideways—I just had to go for it. I'm sure I was pretty keyed up and it was one of those moments where I just visualized the shot I wanted to hit. And it worked. To this day, I'm still amazed I pulled it off. Off a downhill lie with a 4-wood, I hit a low line drive through a gap in the spreading branches of the tree. Now, because of the slope to the green, the ball had to get up. Well, that ball stayed just a yard or so off the ground as it cleared the tree and then began to climb. It went onto the green between two deep bunkers on each side—stopping a few feet from the pin. It sealed the victory for me.

Dad had flown up to Detroit the night before and was following the match. He later said, "I always thought you were a bit of a kook, but when you pulled a wood out for that lie I knew you'd lost your marbles. Nobody in her right mind would even try a shot from that place. There seemed to be no way you could get it up and no way to keep it down under the limbs of the tree." Well, for some reason or another, I was able to visualize the shot and it hit it exactly how I wanted. That happened quite a bit throughout my career. If I saw a shot, I would try to do it. But if I walked up to a shot and had no idea what would happen, I'd play it safe. I wasn't a flamboyant golfer by any means. I just did what I had to do.

It was a great week for sure, but not without one strange incident. The competitors were staying in accommodations in Dearborn Village, owned by the Ford Motor Company. They were individual houses with three floors. Our house had: me; Dad; my best friend and traveling companion, Jean; and Jean's father Mr. Hopkins, who had come up from Cleveland. He had his own room, Dad had a room, and Jean and I shared one up on the top floor. In the middle of the night, somebody tried to get in our bedroom door. I was tired and half asleep and I started for the door while Jean yelled at me, "Don't open that door." Well, come to find out, the cops were chasing somebody, and the fugitive happened to come into our building and was going room to room. There we were, in our PJ's, and it was bedlam for a while. They eventually caught the guy somewhere else. But it just goes to show that the week could have easily turned out much differently. You never know what might have happened.

After her spectacular year in 1947, Louise entered 1948 as the indisputable leading amateur golfer, and recognition of her talents was beginning to go beyond the sports pages. In 1948, she was named one of the 10 young women being given the "Mademoiselle Merit Award" by Mademoiselle Magazine. *Louise was honored, along with the other recipients, by editor-in-chief Betsy Talbot Blackwell at a special ceremony in New York City. The award was designed to recognize a year of "signal achievement" for young women with outstanding careers. In Louise's year, there was a modern dancer, an interior architect, a fashion designer, a Quaker social worker, a lawyer, a pottery craftswoman, an economist, and an educator. Past winners included opera singers, nuclear scientists, novelists, movie stars, and even a resistance leader. Louise told a friend, "I thought I was out of my league with all those other characters. I was scared to death. I looked around that room and thought, 'What the heck am I doing here?'"*

■ ■ ■

Because I had become well known on the national stage, I was fortunate that a number of fun and interesting opportunities came my way. In 1948, I was invited to star alongside Frank Stranahan in a short sports reel called "Muscles and the Lady." It was an eight-minute Sportscope that was shown in movie theaters around the country before the main film. It was produced by RKO Productions and directed by Joe Walsh. I really enjoyed doing it because it was so different from anything else I'd done. Frank was one of the country's top amateur golfers at the time. He was known as "Muscles" because he was a big weight lifter and traveled with bar bells in his luggage so he could exercise wherever he was. He always got a kick out of watching the hotel bell caps trying to lift his bags, unaware that they held all those weights.

Like me, Frank went on to win the British Amateur just a month after we'd shot the movie, and our respective victories helped get the film extra attention. We needed it because it was the first time in years that golf had received any national exposure in the movies. We both had to get permission from the USGA to ensure that nothing infringed on our amateur status, even though we were receiving no pay whatsoever. Apparently, the USGA permitted it because they also thought it would be great publicity for the game of golf.

The movie was narrated by Red Barber, the baseball radio announcer, and featured Frank, as Muscles, dating me, the Lady. The script opened with Frank flying me in his plane into the Boca Raton airport for a golf vacation. As it happened, Frank had been a pilot in the Air Force. His father had founded the Champion Spark Plug Company and they had a company plane, which is the one Frank flew in that scene. As we came in to land, we got about 30 feet off the ground when all of a sudden he said to the co-pilot, "You take it." Well, he turned the controls loose about 15 feet from touchdown and we hit the tarmac with a bang. I swear the plane must have bounced 10 feet back up in the air. When we got out of the plane, all dazed, the director Joe said, "That was a terrible landing, you're going to have to do it again." I said, "You're not getting me back in that plane. No way. You're going to do that without me."

The next scene was at a golf course where Tommy Armour, "The Silver Scot," was sitting in a reclining chair giving us advice on how the game should be played. We then eagerly played a round and hit different kinds of shots based on Tommy's instructions. The film ended in typical Hollywood fashion with me sitting by the pool in a bathing suit and robe admiring Frank in his swimming trunks—flexing his muscles with a bar bell.

The finished film was just eight minutes long after two weeks of shooting. It took that long because we had to film each scene in the same light, which meant there was a lot of sitting around and waiting. At that time, Tommy Armour was teaching at Boca and was great buddies with Joe Kirkwood Sr. and Tony Penna. During our down time, they sat around drinking and telling stories. I was only 24 years old and this was before I drank. And, because Frank was a health nut, he didn't drink either. So he and I would eat ice cream while the other guys drank. My goodness, their stories made my hair stand on end. I learned a bit more about what the guys talk about than I really needed to at that age. All in all, though, it was a really great experience.

Georgia's Always on My Mind

"No other state has been as devastating on the nerves of professional golfers as Georgia, home of Bobby Jones, Louise Suggs and Dorothy Kirby, all amateurs." Bob Harlow, Golf World, *June 25, 1947.*

Golf heritage runs deep and proud in Georgia. The Peach State has given birth to an impressive host of golf champions and is the host to the only men's major championship with a permanent home; The Masters at Augusta National. Georgia has produced so many golfing greats that there were only two years between 1916 to 1930 that the state was without a national championship title (excluding 1917 and 1918 when competition was suspended because of World War I). The Atlanta Journal's *O.B. Keeler called Atlanta the "Golfing Capital of the World." Keeler himself was part of Atlanta's storied history in golf. A legendary sports writer, he traveled over 150,000 miles with fellow Atlantan Bobby Jones, reporting on every one of his competitive rounds and becoming Jones' close friend, confidant, and biographer. Led by the incomparable Jones, Atlanta's golf legends Watts Gunn, Charlie and Dan Yates, Alexa Stirling, and Dorothy Kirby all served as inspiration for the young Louise Suggs as she blossomed into one of Georgia's finest and most heralded athletes. In 1966, she became the first woman in any sport to be elected to the Georgia Sports Hall of Fame. Today, the Georgia communities of Atlanta, Austell, Carrollton, and Sea Island all still proudly claim her as a native daughter. Lithia Springs, where the city of Austell has dedicated a park in Louise's name, Sunset Hills Country Club, Capital City Club, Cherokee Town and Country Club, Eastlake Golf Club, and Sea Island Golf Club all rightfully boast about, and pay tribute to, their long relationships with Louise. The Georgia connection couldn't be stronger, nor a source of greater pride for Louise.*

All of the top amateurs in Georgia during my younger days grew up together on the golf course. The guys never considered

Dot Kirby or me to be women or girls. We were just one of them—competitors. I grew up playing tough men's match play golf, and that helped me later on. My dear friends Charlie and Dan Yates, the Barnes brothers, the three Clay boys, along with Dot and I, were all part of a regular group and we all idolized the previous Atlanta golf generations; starting with Alexa Stirling, then Bobby Jones, Watts Gunn, and Perry Adair. Many came from higher social backgrounds than I did, but they never treated me any differently.

Being from Atlanta, I was, naturally, brought up to revere Bobby Jones. To every Georgia native, he is the greatest that our state ever produced—the embodiment of all that we hold dear in life and in sport. I was too young to see him in his hey-day. In fact, I was only seven when he won the Grand Slam, but all the stories I recall from my childhood centered on that one man—the inspiration to any golf-minded youngster.

I was first introduced to Bobby when I was about seven or eight years old. His father and my grandfather had some kind of business relationship, and my mother went to the same Atlanta high school as his wife, Mary Malone. Of course, once I became old enough to realize who he was, I was completely gaga. I was fortunate to really get to know Bobby when Eastlake Golf Club gave me an honorary membership at the age of 16, after I won the 1940 Georgia State Amateur. I would sit for hours on end at the driving range and watch my hero practice. Every now and again he'd look up and say, "Want to go and play a few?" We'd go out for a few holes, he, of course, with a caddie, and me carrying my own bag. I couldn't afford a caddie even though it was only 38 cents a nine.

There was one moment I remember vividly. We were on the par-3 11th at Eastlake. I asked, "Mr. Jones, if you had one piece of advice for me in golf, what would it be?" He didn't even have to think about it before he replied, "Just hit the heck out of it. It will come down somewhere." Here I was, expecting this expansive dissertation from the great Bobby Jones, but I later realized that he was trying to say all you need to do is hit the golf ball. Don't get all bunged up. Just play golf, Suggs. On another occasion, I was playing with him and ended up behind a tree. I said, "Mr. Jones, what would you do here?" He said, "Well you have four shots. You can go over, under, draw it around the left, or fade it to the right." With that, he threw down four balls and did exactly those four things. I just stood there with my mouth open, thinking how much I wanted to learn to be able to do the same.

There were also a few times at Eastlake on Sundays when he and I would play as partners in what they called the Cat and Dog Fight. Of course at that point, my handicap was scratch and he was plus four, so you know we practically wound up at the bottom of the stack every time. But we did have a lot of fun. I absorbed so much just from watching him and hearing him talk. I picked up all kinds of information that made so much sense and suited my game. My goal was always to emulate him.

I was lucky enough to become his friend and, to this day, one of my most cherished memories is playing with him in an exhibition match right before he retired. It was held at The Highlands Country Club in North Carolina in the summer of 1948, right after I turned professional. Dick Garlington and Dot Kirby made up the foursome. What impressed me the most about his game was his effortless, long-flowing swing. He didn't seem to exert any energy for the results he obtained. It was poetry in motion, with a capital P.

I recently found a copy of a note that I had written to Bobby's dear wife Mary after he died in 1971. It reminded me of how deeply he had affected me. It said, "The golfing world has lost its immortal Bobby, but I have lost a friend and an influence in my life that words cannot describe. Please accept my heartfelt and deepest sympathy."

■ ■ ■

Only twice throughout history have members of the same club played each other in the finals of a USGA championship. Bobby Jones and Watts Gunn, both members of the Atlanta Athletic Club, played each other in the 1925 U.S. Amateur at Oakmont, with Jones prevailing to win his second of five national titles. The other occasion was when Louise Suggs beat Dorothy Kirby two up in 1947 U.S. Women's Amateur at Franklin Hills Country Club in Michigan.

While Bobby Jones was my hero, my great friend and mentor when I was a girl was Dot Kirby. She was four years older than me and quite a player. I really looked up to her. At the age of 12, she became the youngest player to enter a state championship and she was the youngest to win a state title when she won Georgia's at the age of just 13. During her career she won a U.S. Women's Amateur, five Georgia State titles, a North & South, a Southern, and two Titleholders. No doubt, I put Dot on a pedestal. She was very elegant and much more sophisticated than me. When I was about 14 years old, she invited me to go to a Saturday matinee in Atlanta at the Loew's Grand. I was so excited I didn't sleep the night before. I couldn't stop talking about it until finally Mom joked, "Would you stop talking about it? I know as much about Dot Kirby as you do." I thought she was something on a stick, and she really was to me. It would be fair to say that she was my idol.

While we were friends, we had a healthy rivalry, which made each of us a better golfer. Dot and I were both honorary members of Capital City Club. Every afternoon in the summer, after we got off work, we'd go and play nine holes or we'd practice beside each other and just talk about golf. We played a lot of exhibitions in Georgia for various clubs and charities. And while we were certainly good pals, when it came to competition, we would really hunker down and try to win against each other.

During 1947, Atlanta hosted both the Western Open at Capital City and the Southern Amateur at Eastlake. I happened to win them both and was thrilled that Bobby Jones presented the trophy at the Southern. Unfortunately, Dot was left as runner-up in both of them. I guess I was just a bulldog. If I'm going to play you, you're not my friend while I'm playing you. That same year, I beat Dot in the 36-hole final of the U.S. Amateur. Afterwards, the media asked me about why two good friends like us wouldn't talk during the match. I told them it's best not to talk because conversation can take your mind off the game when you need to concentrate. Even the smallest comment, like "nice shot" can be taken as either envy or sarcasm. The best way not to be misunderstood is to not say anything.

The New York Daily News' *Bob Brumby said, "To Dorothy, golf is a game, but to Louise it is a challenge. A challenge that must be met with every ounce of strength in her shapely little body."*

As I said to my great friend Jean Hopkins, and this is something I said only to Jean and Dot, "When we're in this match, we're not friends." Jean always said, "If it hadn't been for you, I could have won some stuff." Unfortunately, it was the same for Dot. She never turned professional, and that was just as well because she didn't have the killer instinct. You've got to have a little bit of a mean streak in you and she was too nice. Instead, she focused on broadcasting and went on to be a radio announcer for Atlanta's WGST. Eventually, she took a chance on TV when it first started. If the Golf Channel had been available in her era, she'd have been like Kelly Tilghman. She was really ahead of her time and did one of the first live broadcasts from the Titleholders. By then, she was with WSB in Atlanta, which later became an NBC affiliate. She wound up as an executive vice president in marketing and sales.

When Louise beat Dot Kirby 5 & 4 in the final of the 1948 Doherty Challenge Cup, her third Doherty win in four years, it was the fourth time in eight months that Louise had beaten her Atlanta friend in the final of an important tournament.

■　■　■

During the years after Dad opened the course at Lithia Springs, a group of guys would frequently drive an hour from Carrollton in west Georgia to play Lithia because it was the only course in the area. Carrollton is the county seat of Carroll County and, at that time, had a population of about 10,000. It was originally a cotton-producing town but ultimately diversified into lumber, hosiery, shoe production, and cloth mills. It also became the nation's largest pimento producer and home to the University of West Georgia. Eventually, after Grandfather Spiller died in 1946, that same group from Carrollton convinced Dad to come to Carrollton and help build a nine-hole course on a Robert Trent Jones design.

Dad plowed the land, cleared the trees, blasted the ditches, bulldozed the red Georgia clay to mold the greens, seeded them with Bermuda grass, put in two artificial ponds, and oversaw the progress of the new clubhouse. He worked his behind off until the course opened in July 1948. It became Sunset Hills Country Club and later expanded to 18 holes.

Two hundred and twenty locals joined the club for an annual subscription of $60. Dad later became the club's pro, looking after the course and the caddies, and Mom helped out in the pro shop and generally made everyone feel at home. Dad had such a commitment to detail and a hands-on approach that he himself went out into the woods and dug up pink and white dogwood trees and alternately planted them in a circle in front to the club. They were quite beautiful and I'm sorry to see them gone now.

Mom and Dad were beloved in Carrollton. Everyone knew that Dad had his own level of fame from baseball, but they loved that he never lost his common touch. My parents really made the club a wonderful place to be. I would have to say, Mom was really happy in Carrollton. She had a lot of friends and played bridge with them often.

Dad and me outside the Sunset Hills clubhouse. Photo by Birdsong Studio.

Because I had turned professional in 1948, Sunset Hills became my family base when I was traveling. It was an important hub for me to come home to, for rest and a tune-up, because nobody was around to bother me. I could come and go as I pleased, hit golf balls, and play all over the golf course. In those days, not too many women played and men only played on Wednesdays, Saturdays, and Sundays, so the rest of the time the course was clear. I played with the members quite a bit and that's were I got in some competitive practice. When the club opened, I was honored when they rolled out the red carpet for me to take part in the grand opening. Four hundred locals showed up to watch me hit shots—with my brother Rell catching them as he'd done so many times when I practiced at Lithia Springs.

A couple of years later, in 1950, Dad and I decided it would be great for the club, the city, and the LPGA if we could host a tournament for the girls. So, we went to some of the members and persuaded them to help us. The first Carrollton Open was held in September 1950 at Sunset Hills. The city and local neighborhoods were enthusiastic and folks turned out in droves to both help organize the event and witness the festivities. Dad and I helped beat the bushes, with the members helping raise the $5,000 needed to run the tournament, which offered a purse fund of $3,500 with a first prize of $750—fifty of the Carrollton businessmen gave $100 each. Wives on the entertainment committee got baby sitters for their children so that they could help serve meals to the golfers, while various groups from around town put on special events like luncheons and cookouts, and folks also opened up their homes to the players. Such was the anticipation that you couldn't walk into a store without someone asking about your involvement in the week's events. The girls didn't have to spend a dime except for caddies and gasoline. It was a complete community tournament and made Carrollton proud as it brought nationwide attention to the town when the big guns in women's golf came to play. It was the first of its kind for the LPGA and became somewhat of a model going forward. It was really gratifying to see how it all came together.

The day before the players were due to arrive for the tournament, Babe called Dad and said, "Johnny, I gotta have a little pocket change," which of course wasn't allowed by the LPGA—then or now. Despite that rule, Babe would still try to get appearance fees and then always claim she gave it right back to the LPGA. Dad played dumb and he came to me and said, "What should I do?" I told him I'd fix it, which I did by calling Plug Osborne, her boss at Wilson. I said, "Plug, this is what happened, and she's so darned dumb that she called my Dad and asked him for money. What do you think he's going to say to her? And, she had already promised me that she would come here when we got the tournament together." Well, I don't know what Plug did but she was there the next day, along with her husband George Zaharias, who was well known as a professional wrestler.

The first day of the tournament got underway and, since Sunset Hills at the time was only nine holes with a par of 37 over 3,155 yards, we played it twice from different tees. After one round, Babe and I were tied for the lead with three-under 71.

Everything was going quite well, with the exception of a couple of uncomfortable moments with Babe's husband. Georgia was a dry state back then, but Dad had somehow managed to get some liquor and beer. He put some bourbon, scotch, gin, and vodka in the girls' locker room, which was actually the men's locker room because the ladies' locker room wasn't big enough for the golf tournament. Well, I walked into the locker room and George was in there putting all this booze in his pockets. I said, "George, what the heck are you doing in here? This is the ladies' locker room. And what are you doing stealing the liquor?" He stammered, "Well, I didn't think you girls needed it and I can use it more." When I told him to put it back, he started to argue with me. I said, "If you argue with me, I'll go and get my father." Well, Dad knew George from the days when my grand folks had the ballpark and George and his brother used to wrestle as part of the entertainment schedule. I think he was a little bit afraid of Dad because Dad didn't take anything from anybody. He put it back. Later, Dad took it and put it in his locker and gave me the key for when the girls wanted anything.

That first night after we played, there was a lot of fun as everybody sat around and sang and played in the clubhouse. The club was really the social center of town so a lot of members were there as well. Now, this was in the days of no air conditioning, and it was pretty hot so we had a bunch of fans going and all the windows open. There was good food, cooked by all the wives, and it was really just a happy time. Bev Hanson played the piano beautifully, and her brother Gordon, who was on Broadway at that time, began singing along with her. They both had beautiful voices. Babe played the harmonica pretty well and eventually everyone began joining in, singing, and having a great time.

Meanwhile, George had helped himself to more than enough liquor. It was hot and sweltering in the clubhouse and all of a sudden George took his shirt off right there in the clubhouse dining room. He had no under shirt on, and so here's this big guy sweating up a storm. Dad went over to him and said, "George, put your shirt on." To that, George replied, "What for? It's hot in here." Dad, a little louder this time, said, "Put your shirt on George. You're in the country club on a Saturday night. You don't even take your shirt off in the daytime here." At this point, George started getting belligerent and Dad was just plain mad. To be honest, I didn't know what was going to happen. Well, Dad went downstairs to the pro shop and came back with his shotgun. He walked up to George and said, "George, I said put your shirt on." George looked at him and asked, "You wouldn't use that thing, would you, Johnny?" Dad said, "You know me, George." Well, not another word needed to be said. George put his shirt on in a hurry and that was the end of it. Babe had always described her husband perfectly. She used to say, "When I married George, he weighed 150 and looked like a Greek god. Now he weighs 300 and looks like a goddamn Greek." He was from Cripple Creek, Colorado, and was known in the wrestling world as "The Crying Greek from Cripple Creek."

Despite that moment, we still had a great time. One song just seemed to lead to another and we ended up having to kick everyone out because we had to play the next day. Babe went on to shoot 82 and I led by one shot from Patty Berg. However, Patty ended beating me on the third and last day with a 72 to my 74. It was hard to be a hostess, with the attention of the whole town on you, while still playing well.

A year later at the second LPGA tourney in Carrollton, coming down the stretch it looked like Babe might win. Knowing this, I hit a good final drive on the 18th, leaving me with a 200-yard approach shot that was over water to a pin tucked behind a bunker. There was only about 10 feet between the bunker and the hole. I was in the middle of the fairway, pulled out my 4-wood, and hit a great shot that just kissed the cup and ended a few inches away. I tapped in and that left Babe needing to match my birdie to force a playoff. She hit a great drive, right over the line of the dogleg and over the famous red barn. However, her second shot didn't hold the green and her chip came up 18 inches short, giving me the win. In 2006, the club placed a bronze plaque on the spot from where I hit that shot. I was so grateful when they also made me an honorary member.

Today, I still have a fond attachment to Sunset Hills. Each year, the club hosts the Georgia Women's Match Play Championship and the trophy is a silver flower bowl I gave to the club. It is a piece I had won and which had been presented to me by Bobby Jones when I won the 1947 Southern Amateur.

The silver flower bowl is perpetually on show in a glass-door case in Sunset Hills' clubhouse. It is part of a larger display that pays tribute to Louise, an initiative that was spearheaded by Sunset Hills' member Betty Rich, a long-time USGA volunteer and self-confessed "biggest fan" of Louise.

That bowl was Mom's favorite piece, one that she would put fresh daffodils in during each spring. It means a lot to me that it has found a permanent home with a good purpose.

■　■　■

The city of Atlanta has always been so good to me. I've seen it grow and change so much over the decades, but I haven't lost any of my love for it. At one point, in recognition of my achievements, Governor Melvin Thompson made me an Honorary Lieutenant Colonel in the Georgia Militia. The honor carried with it the Honor of Aid to the Governor. I got a license tag that said "Governor's Staff" to put on my car, and with it I could park anywhere in Atlanta or Georgia and never get a ticket. When I showed it to my parents, Dad said, "What are you going do with that thing?" To which I said, "I thought I'd put it on the car." He told me, "If you put that on the car you can just move out of the house right now." It didn't surprise me because I knew he didn't believe in those kinds of perks. He believed you had to earn them. I saw his point and I didn't put it on my car.

■　■　■

There are three clubs in Atlanta that are dear to my heart and played an important part in my golf career. Eastlake Golf Course is the legendary home course of Bobby Jones and the oldest golf course in Atlanta. They gave me an honorary membership when I was 16. In addition to Bobby, most of Atlanta's great players were members there: Charles and Dan Yates, Alexa Stirling, Dot Kirby, Watts Gunn, and Dan's son, Danny Yates.

Stewart Maiden, a highly regarded Scottish professional, was the teaching pro at Eastlake and was Bobby Jones' swing coach. Before I became a member and was still in high school, O.B. Keeler had noticed my game and asked Stewart if he'd come to Austell and watch me hit a few shots, which he did. Quite frankly, it surprised me that he came, but I wasn't old enough or smart enough to adequately realize the caliber of who he was at the time. Because Dot Kirby was O.B.'s favorite girl, so to speak, I think O.B. just wanted to find out what Stewart thought about the way I hit the ball. He thought her golf game was better while O.B.'s wife, Ma Keeler, thought mine was better. I never really heard what Stewart thought. He checked my grip and said, "Lassie, always check your grip. You can put the ball anywhere you want in your stance, but if your grip is good, you can move your hands to get the ball moving any way you want it to go. If you can move your hands quickly enough, you can get out of any jam." That's when I first really began thinking about hands. And to this day, I still believe that the golf swing begins with a good grip.

■ ■ ■

Capital City Club also was generous enough to give me an honorary membership after I won the Georgia State title in 1940. Capital City has hosted five Georgia State Amateur Championships, five Georgia State Women's Amateur, two Women's Western Opens (both of which I won), a Southern Amateur, a Women's Southern Amateur, and the PGA Tour World Golf Championship. It also had an impressive list of members including the Yates family, Harvey Ward, Jim Gabrielson, Billy Andrade, and Dot Kirby. Before I became a member, it was the first really nice course I had seen outside of Lithia Springs.

On March 14, 1948, at Capital City Club, an exhibition charity match featured professionals Babe Zaharias and Patty Berg against amateurs Louise and Dot Kirby. According to Golf World, *"Never before, even in the days when Bob Jones was King, have Atlanta citizens turned out as they did on Sunday to witness four gals swap strokes in a pro-amateur four-ball." The media, of course, hyped up the rivalry between Louise and Babe, which, in turn, drove throngs of fans and clogged up the local roads with traffic jams—all to pay the $5 entry which generated $25,000 for the Mountain School for Girls in Tallulah Falls, Georgia. At the time, it was believed to be the largest one-day take in the history of Atlanta golf. Babe and Patty prevailed on the 17th hole. The media tried to determine the stroke play score of each player but had difficulty because of the number of putts given. A general consensus was reached that Babe shot 71; Louise, 73; Patty, 74; and Dot Kirby, 75. However, as* Golf World *reported, "The Babe, who never gives herself the worst of it when it comes to figuring out medal play score, announced over the loud speaker that she had made a 69."*

■ ■ ■

In 1956, I joined a number of other Atlanta folks as one of the original members of Cherokee Town and Country Club. A number of years later, in recognition of my career, the club was kind enough to offer me lifetime honorary membership. However, when I heard that honorary members don't get voting privileges, I politely declined the offer and said I'd prefer to pay dues and maintain my voice in the club. I heard that the Cherokee board then changed its policy because they very much wanted to be able to honor me. As a result, I became the first person ever to become an honorary member and keep my voting rights.

Cherokee has one of the most impressive displays of Louise Suggs memorabilia and historical artifacts in a library that was opened in conjunction with Louise becoming an honorary member. The Louise Suggs Library was the inspiration of Cherokee member Wayne Aaron, a former Ford Motor Company executive and member of the USGA's Museum Committee. Aaron and his wife Claudia both share a tremendous passion for golf's history and collectibles. After they moved from New Jersey to Atlanta and joined Cherokee in 1988, Wayne's voracious interest in the history of golf led him to look into his new club's past.

"I asked several Cherokee members, 'Who is the most famous golfer our club has ever had?'" said Aaron. "They thought and thought, and a couple of them said, 'I'm not sure we've ever really had one.' Then I asked a couple of board members and one said, 'I think one of our earlier members won an Atlanta area amateur event, but I just can't remember his name.' I finally got myself a membership directory and I'm flipping through to see if I know anybody, and I recognized a couple of people. By the time I got to the S's, I looked down and there's 'Ms. Louise Suggs'. I said, 'Get out of here. This can't be the same one. It must be someone else.' I approached John Jordan, the club's long time general manager. I said, 'John, is this THE Louise Suggs, or someone else?' He verified, 'Oh no, that's THE Louise. She's one of our early, early members.' I was like, 'My God, where's the bronze statue at the front of the club for this

woman?' That's when I went on my mission to track Louise down, and she was very gracious."

Aaron's skill and passion for tracking down historical pieces kicked into full gear. In fact, he did such a thorough job, the original U.S. Women's Open Championship trophy is cased at Cherokee. The first U.S. Women's Open in 1946 came under the jurisdiction of the fledgling WPGA and the Spokane Athletic Round Table. Louise won the title twice, in 1949 and 1952, before the USGA agreed to take ownership of the Championship in 1953. As such, Louise called the Spokane group in Tacoma and asked what to do with the trophy. She was told, "Well, whose is the last name on it?" It was, of course, Louise, and so she was told, "Well, then it's yours." All those years later, Louise gave it to Cherokee to be part of the display in the library room named in her honor.

This life-size portrait was commissioned by Cherokee and was unveiled in conjunction with the opening of the Louise Suggs Library.
Photo courtesy Cherokee Town and Country Club.

Sea Island—Home Away from Home

My fondness and loyalty to Georgia is profound, and today the true heart of my love for the Peach State rests on the coast in the Golden Isles—Sea Island. For over 60 years now, Sea Island has been my home away from home. While my primary residence has been in Florida, I've kept a home on Sea Island. And always will. So many folks there are family to me. The entire area has always represented such a peaceful and happy reprieve, and I've always tried to go and spend time there as often as I can, and for as long as I can. I've known generations of families who've grown up and moved through there—from the wonderful Jones family who built up the famed resort in the 1920's, to the countless people working in the lodge, the golf clubs, and the beach club. And I can't forget generations of members and their families.

Some of my dearest friends, like Pat and Cartan Clarke, and Bill Jones III and his wife Sally, still live on the Golden Isles. I became friends with former First Couple George and Barbara Bush there, and it's where I met Cari Gardner and her three wonderful sons. Cari and I became friends when we both worked at the Sea Island Golf Club Learning Center. We have been through a lot together in life—good and not so good. Cari is really much like my own daughter and I truly consider her, Steve, Chris and Jason to be my family. Such have been the blessings of my connection with the island.

I first went to Sea Island in the spring of 1948 when I was 24. I had been named to the Curtis Cup team and, like the rest of the team, had planned to stay and play in the British Ladies Amateur a week later. A friend of mine, Freeman Darby, had suggested that Sea Island would be a great place to get a feel of what it's like to play near the ocean, with the wind, etc., so that's what I did. There is no doubt that those drives back and forth to Sea Island paid off in how I deal with playing in tricky weather.

I came back to Sea Island in 1953 when I was playing on the LPGA Tour. I said to Irv Harned, who was the manager there at the time, "Why don't you put on an LPGA tournament?" He liked the idea and talked it through with Bill Jones, Sr. and from there, Sea Island agreed to put up the money and stage the first event of the LPGA season that next January. It was held from 1954 to 1963. I won the first event, and then won again in 1961.

Because it was the first tournament of the year, the Sea Island Open got quite a bit of publicity, which pleased me and everyone else on Sea Island. But boy, it was cold in January of that first year. We had charcoal pots on the tees to give us a chance to warm our hands between each hole. Phyllis Semple, Carol Semple Thompson's mother, had on one of those plastic rain jackets—a new thing in those days. It was so cold though, that thing just crumbled and fell into a million pieces.

Irv also came up with this idea to make the spectators feel welcome—he called it "The Men in the Red Hats." Basically, there were 15 Sea Island members that agreed to wear these bright red hats and they were whom the spectators were told to ask questions if they needed help. When Dad came over from Atlanta, Irv gave him one to wear. Dad wondered, "If anybody asks me a question, what am I going to say?" Irv said, "You'll think of something," which we all knew Dad would.

After I won the first Sea Island Open in 1954, Bill Jones, Sr. told me, "Come and do some teaching when you're not on Tour. Be with the Sea Island folks and this will be your home." It was a wonderful offer and, by accepting, I became the club's first touring professional. I kind of knew that Sea Island was a place to where I could always come back. It was like my security blanket. Our agreement was sealed with a handshake, and right up to today it is still representative of the wonderful relationship I've always had with the Jones family. Bill Jones III, who I watched grow from a little boy to become chairman of the resort, still treats me with the same warmth and generous spirit.

Bill Jones III said, "When Louise made the handshake agreement with my grandfather to come to Sea Island, it really wasn't a business relationship. It was more like she joined our family. We've been blessed to have Louise not only as part of Sea Island, but as part of our lives. Here you have this iconic personality who doesn't act that way. She's someone you want to be like. She's a straight shooter and you know exactly where you stand with Louise. There's never any pretension or games. The thing I love about Louise is that she treats all people the same. I've witnessed it so many times. She just makes people feel so comfortable. You don't have to spend much time with her at all to feel that way. Former First Lady Barbara Bush and Louise became fast friends through Sea Island, but her friends are also waiters and waitresses, doormen, cleaners—because all people are the same to Louise."

Under Bill Jones III's direction, Sea Island underwent a $100,000 project to have replicas of all of Louise's trophies made. The display, which is still proudly on show, was unveiled on October 7, 2003, shortly after Louise's 80th birthday.

■ ■ ■

Before Sea Island underwent considerable renovations, my accommodation at the resort was in a dormitory-style building. It was a lovely set-up, which worked perfectly given how much I traveled back and forth from the island. The same building was used to house the college kids who were hired as summer interns. Their job was to host the kids of families staying at the resort. They'd take care of and entertain the kids with things like movies, swim meets, sailing, and all sorts of other activities. You could almost say they

I became dear friends with George and Barbara Bush because of our mutual connection to Sea Island.

were like babysitters. For the most part, they were the teenage sons and daughters of the members and I knew many of their parents and even grandparents. Jack Nicklaus' daughter, Nancy, a lovely young woman, worked there one summer.

Well, as good as the kids were, they were still kids and could get pretty rambunctious without mom and dad around. One night, everything was fairly quiet and I was sitting in my room reading a book when all of a sudden I heard this tremendous racket. It sounded unlike anything I had ever heard before and I couldn't imagine what it was. My room was at one end of the hall and I poked my head out of my door to see, down at the far end, four young men hitting golf balls. I was only in my robe, but went back in my room and got a golf club and wielded it as I walked out the door. I said, "If anyone wants to play rough, I'm ready." That stopped that little shebang—but not before they cracked a window in the door. I can't count on how many other occasions they set off the sprinkler systems—at one point, the water ruined a bunch of computers down in the office. Fortunately, my system wasn't on the same line as theirs so I never got wet.

There was one particular moment though that took the biscuit. It was Christmas Eve. My friend Jean and I were dressed and getting ready to go over to the hotel for dinner. We walked out of our room all dazzled up and what not, only to see this young guy come flying out of another room with nothing on but a jock strap. Before I could even think, here came a girl without a stitch of clothing. It really makes me laugh to think back on it. But there were plenty of times when it just wasn't funny.

Some of the kids were worse than others and really had no respect for the place when they tore it up. It was hard to imagine that they came from some of the families they did. They were in college and should have known better. With that said, they were just kids and after a hard day's work they just wanted to put on blue jeans and a t-shirt and go out honky-tonking until the early hours of the morning, wake up, and do it all over again. After a while, I think they got the message not to rattle me around too much. But I'd have to admit that I enjoyed being around the young ones. It was a fascinating experience for me and, in many ways, I felt like I practically raised some of them.

■ ■ ■

Many of Louise's closest friends from Sea Island came from her teaching days at Sea Island Golf Club's Learning Center. Pat Clarke was one of those. Pat and her husband Cartan are Sea Island members, and Pat, for many years, was closely involved with USGA activities, including serving six years on the USGA Women's Committee. She remembers, "Louise was so worried that she was much too rough and strict with those kids in the dorm area when they'd get up to their hanky panky. She was always afraid she'd hurt somebody's feelings, even though there were times she wanted to kill these kids. One night, after I had taken her back to her apartment, she called me back because she was having a little heart trouble. I zoomed back and got an ambulance to take her off to the hospital and I followed in the car. Well, let me say, those kids were so upset that the woman who regularly rattled their cage and gave them such hell was in trouble. It showed how much they adored her—absolutely would have done anything for her. It was touching to see that rowdy group care so deeply.

"As great as Louise has been on the golf course, it's not as well-known that she is quite a teacher. She is an honorary member of the LPGA's teaching group. That's how I got to know her. Cartan and I had moved from Minnesota down to Atlanta, and I was feeling awfully sorry for myself. My mother had a house on Sea Island, so Cartan persuaded me to spend a little time there. I finished playing golf one day and I happened to see that Louise Suggs had a clinic, which I quickly signed up for. It was going to be an all-week affair, I thought that was heaven sent, and I got all excited in preparation for it. I got there on the first day and went out to the practice tee—extremely nervous. Out she came, alone, and I said, 'Where is everybody?' She replied, 'You're it!' To which I said, 'I thought you were having a clinic.' Louise laughed and said, 'I was but you're the only one who showed up.' So, for four days I was in this clinic alone with the great Louise Suggs. I've never been so nervous in my life as I was when I first had to hit balls in front of her. However, I quickly found that she had the most incredible knack for making you feel at ease. On the first day, she asked if I'd like to have lunch, which I did, and I found her so comfortable to be with that I got over my terrible nervousness of being the only one in this clinic with this very famous woman.

"That first afternoon, she tweaked just a few things and all of a sudden my shots were just soaring. She teaches you as you are. She takes the body that the Lord gave you and the swing that you've got and she brings her expertise to that and, all of a sudden, things begin to gel. I started hitting golf balls that I'd never hit in my life. I've never had such a glorious time. In my later years, I got my greatest enjoyment from golf because of that clinic that nobody showed up for. That's really where our great friendship

began. If she could put up with my swing, alone for a week, she could put up with anything.

"Louise is like a multi-faceted diamond. You never know what part of that diamond is going to show up. One of those sides is a wonderful sense of humor. When Louise won the USGA Bob Jones Award in 2007, Sea Island had an event to honor her. We called it 'Fireside Chat With Louise Suggs.' We set it up where she and I each had a microphone, and I was to ask Louise questions, to prompt some of her stories. As we were getting ready to go up the step to our chairs, I said, 'Here we go Louise, to our fireside chat.' She stopped in her tracks, looked me dead in the eye in front of everyone and she said, 'Now you know I'm not a Democrat!' I laughed, 'Geez, Louise.' She obviously was joking about the Fireside Chats President Roosevelt gave in the 1930's to calm the nation."

The deep and enduring friendship with Cari Gardner was also borne out of Louise's teaching days on the island. According to Cari, "I affectionately call Louise Ladybug. Have you ever looked at a ladybug? They're tough, they've got these hard shells, but they're beautiful. Louise is more than a friend to me—she's my family. She knew me from my comings and goings in the pro shop where I worked during my early 20's. Later, after Davis Love Jr. and others in our Sea Island family were killed in a plane crash, I was asked if I'd move to the new Learning Center where Louise was one of the instructors. She was in her 60's by then and she was teaching non-stop from sun up to sundown. I noticed that she couldn't say no to anyone and there was a wait-list to get a lesson from Louise Suggs. She never sat when she taught and when she taught kids, she'd even tee the ball up for them. One day, she came in all red faced and sat down. I said, 'That's it! You're over-doing it. Why? You don't need to. We're going to cut back your hours, so give me your appointment book.' With that, I took her book and cut back on the number of lessons she gave. I had to take this line with her since she wouldn't say 'no.' She's a driver and doesn't like to disappoint people. She's got a heart of gold.

"Louise is an amazing teacher. She makes it so simple. I will never forget when **Southern Living** *magazine came in to do an article on her.*

She wanted me to be her student for the photo shoot. The photographer said, 'Give her a lesson and forget I'm here.' So, I'm standing over the ball, I've got my grip, and Louise said to me, 'Look at the face of your club.' We're both bent over looking and she said again, 'Cari, look at the face of your club.' She started to get fussy and raised her voice this time. 'Cari, look at the face of your club,' until I finally said, 'I would if you'd move your head.' It was so comical we started laughing and giggling.

■ ■ ■

I feel so honored to be able to call George and Barbara Bush my friends. Barbara and I became especially good friends after I gave her a couple of lessons while George was still in office. They had honeymooned on Sea Island when they married in 1945 and would celebrate some of their wedding anniversaries on the island. We would laugh about the fact that we first got to know each other because George had given a lesson with me to her as an anniversary gift. In retrospect, I'm so glad he gave it to her because it marked the beginning of a great friendship.

There was one particular day that still makes me chuckle. I was with the Bushes, getting ready to play at Ocean Forest Golf Club. I have to say that George plays golf the way I like to play the game. It's like a racetrack for him. He just hits and goes. On this occasion, I was on the practice tee warming up and George was on one side of me while Barbara was on the other. I made a swing suggestion to Barbara and she sharply said, "You told me that before," to which I replied, "Do it then." George was so taken aback, he laughed, "You're the only one who's ever been able to get away with that." She laughed too. Barbara really is quite an amazing woman. And, an extremely strong person. When I was teaching her, she wanted to know exactly why she had to do the things I was trying to teach her. I respect that.

*Barbara Bush and I watched George play at Ocean Forest Golf Club on
Sea Island (accompanied by my poodle, Damit).*

As I got closer to the Bushes, it began to occur to me what little
privacy they had, both in and out of office. One day, we were going
to play and we'd left my clubs on the cart with Barbara's. I came
around the corner and saw this guy with my golf bag upside down.
Instinctively, I yelled, "Hey, what are you doing?" I didn't realize
that it was a Secret Service guy. He calmly said, "You don't want to
get blown up do you? We have to check everything." And he did
the same to Barbara's bag. It's frightening, in a sense, to realize how
necessary that is.

One time, my friends Fran Green and Caroline Carter made
up a foursome with Barbara and me at the Sea Island Golf Course.
Fran's husband came out to greet us. All of a sudden, as he was

walking towards Fran, this Secret Service guy got in between them and said, "Sir, you're not allowed." That same kind of security was on full show during another game. Barbara and I were playing and she said, "I'm hitting it terribly—I quit! Let's go and find George and heckle him." So, that's what we did. I was driving the cart while Barbara was sitting back with her feet up on the dash. All of a sudden, she sat bolt upright and started looking around. She exclaimed, "They all couldn't have gone to the bathroom at the same time!" I was unaware, but she had noticed that six or so Secret Service guys had converged and, all at once, went into the nearby bushes. Turns out, there was someone in there. Her Secret Service guy came up afterward and said, "I just wanted to tell you, Mrs. Bush, that he didn't have a gun." George just kept playing even though it happened right in front of him, and it occurred to me that most of us have no idea the kind of security those folks need all the time. Meanwhile, the Bushes would just go about their daily business and handle things like this with their usual grace and class.

■　■　■

I happen to love music of all kinds. But much of today's pop music is beyond me. One day, Bill Jones came to me all excited, and said that I was going to give a lesson to Lisa Loeb at Ocean Forest Golf Club. Quite frankly, I had to admit I didn't know who she was. I found out that she's a Grammy-nominated singer songwriter with a platinum number one hit. Her boyfriend at the time was another musician, Dweezil Zappa, and a friend of Davis Love III. Like a lot of kids at Sea Island, I've known Davis since he was a little boy. I was a friend of his father Davis Love Jr., who died in the 1988 plane crash that took the lives of some other dear Sea Island friends and teachers, John Popa and Jimmy Hodges—a tremendous tragedy that rocked all of us in the Sea Island community.

When I first met Lisa, I discovered that she was extremely talented and coordinated, which surprised me and, I think, her too. After the lesson, we went to the clubhouse for a beer and I told her that I was 75 and was going to New York to spend Christmas by myself at The Plaza. Well, that Christmas Eve, the concierge at The Plaza called and asked what I wanted for my special Christmas breakfast—courtesy of Lisa Loeb. She left no forwarding phone number or address for me to thank her. So, I went over to the record store at Trump Plaza and bought a bunch of her CD's right then and there. To this day, I still haven't been able to express my gratitude to her.

■ ■ ■

Giving back is an important concept for me. I'm so grateful for the help and friendships I've had along the way. Unfortunately, the trappings of my career didn't put me in a position where I could do something like set up a foundation, but I always wanted to do as much as I could when asked. With that, I was thrilled to be part of a charity called Suggs Superstars on the Golden Isles. It was something started a number of years ago by Marla and Dick Grote, a couple from Cincinnati. They had a house on Sea Island and decided to try and help underprivileged children by encouraging them stay in school and go on to college. Marla and Dick came to me and asked me if they could use my name and call it Suggs Superstars. Of course, I didn't hesitate. If the kids stayed in school from fourth grade through the eighth, we would help them with college scholarships. We took only 25 students, who were required to keep up a certain grade average to stay in the program. We had a representative at the school so that we knew they were studying and were in class when they were supposed to be. In addition to the Grotes' donations, we had tournaments and events to help funding, and we would encourage other Sea Island members to give money.

I would occasionally go visit the kids at school. Unless you were sick, if you missed school you'd be kicked out. There was one time when nobody realized just how sick one of our little girls had been. She passed away during the night and they found her in bed the next morning. Her obituary read that she was a member of Suggs Superstars. I can't tell you how much that really impacted me. It broke my heart.

Dick and Marla did so much for those kids. When Dick died, his company sent the plane down from Cincinnati and took all our kids up to sing at his funeral. That's how much he and Marla meant to the community.

■ ■ ■

There is no greater testimonial to the essence of Louise Suggs and how she views and treats people around her than the relationships that have endured over her years at Sea Island. While she's built friendships with millionaire businessmen, former Presidents and First Ladies, and global celebrities alike, Louise doesn't see their fame or stature. To her, they're just people. The common denominator for Louise is simple; are they good folks? If they are, they make the cut. And so Louise's friends at Sea Island include a host of longtime staff throughout the resort. At the top of that list is Charlesetta Cross. Born and raised on Sea Island, Charlesetta has worked at Sea Island for over 40 years in various capacities. She is now head of housekeeping at Ocean Forest Golf Club, where Louise now has her Sea Island accommodations. "I was 20 years old when I started working at Sea Island and met Ms. Suggs. She was staying in the dorm rooms at The Cloister, where the kids who worked at Sea Island in the summer would stay. I started taking care of her suite when she was in town and we struck up a relationship from there. Ms. Suggs always had this real sweet demeanor about her, even when the kids upstairs were making a lot of noise. She has always had this mildness. Now, after all these years, she's like the matriarch at Ocean Forest."

In 2010, Louise tripped and fell early one morning outside her suite at Ocean Forest while walking her beloved toy poodle, Damit. She hit her head badly and sustained life-threatening injuries. As the medics loaded Louise into the ambulance, the Ocean Forest staff gathered around in hushed and nervous silence. Louise would later say that the last thing she remembered in the ambulance before being rushed to the emergency room was the sight of Charlesetta holding Damit close to the ambulance window. It was Charlesetta's way of letting her know they had her back. Always.

"I know Damit needs to be with her and we all know how she feels about him. I was worried he wasn't going to make it if something happened to her. The dog is her heart. He tickles me sometimes. He allows me to come in to her room but I have to ask him. I've learned to knock on her door and say, "Damit, can I come in?" Once he hears my voice he's okay, but he still won't let me get close to her until he decides it's all right. He's so protective over her. And that's a good thing."

It turns out, the whole Sea Island community is protective over Louise. And that's a good thing.

A Great Moment in Great Britain

In April 1948, a month before leaving for Britain to represent the U.S. in the Curtis Cup and then compete in the British Ladies' Amateur, Louise won the North & South Women's Championship at Pinehurst. She beat fellow Curtis Cupper Grace Lenczyk 2&1 in the final in front of what was considered to be the largest gallery ever for women's golf at Pinehurst. Louise had lost this title the year before to Babe Zaharias on the 20th hole and speculation was already spreading that Louise would soon turn professional. The media began to escalate the potential rivalry between Babe and Louise. They were foreseeing a series of matches that many believed would even outdraw the crowds of a U.S. Women's Open. The rivalry was considered a natural—certain to garner the attention of the world. But before the sports world would get its dream match, the icing on the cake for one of golf's greatest amateur careers was waiting for Louise in the British Isles.

Don't ask me why, but some the greatest moments in my life have happened during terrible weather. I met my fiancé Mac because we were dodging some awful rain on the golf course, and many of my best tournament rounds and wins came in conditions that sent most folks inside to shelter. My weeks in Great Britain for the 1948 Curtis Cup Matches and the British Ladies' Amateur Championship were no different—I was on the winning U.S. Curtis Cup team and then a week later became champion at the British Ladies, which stands out as the proudest moment of my career. And guess what? To say the weather was appalling would be a gross understatement.

I was tremendously excited to head to Britain—my first trip out of the country. I felt that I'd accomplished pretty much what I could in the U.S. As there wasn't a prestigious championship in the U.S. that I hadn't won at least once, if not two or three times, this was going to be a whole new challenge for me. The U.S. Curtis Cup team had been picked in January of 1948 and we pretty much all knew each other, bonding during the various top amateur championships running up to our scheduled departure in May. Our last event, a couple of weeks before shipping out, was the North & South Women's Championship at Pinehurst, which I won that year for the third time. We were all making final preparations, including getting our passports squared away when, at the last minute, we hit a snafu with mine. When I sent in my application, as Mae Louise Suggs, I didn't notice that the doctor had spelled my name May on my birth certificate. Because of that, my paperwork was sent back unprocessed from the passport office. Needless to say, it made me gulp. It seemed that there really wasn't time to get it turned around again. Luckily for me, Ma Keeler was there and she knew Homer Cummins, the former United States Attorney General. Coincidentally, he presented me the trophy for the Championship that same week. It turned out that a friend of his was the head of the passport outfit in Washington and, believe it or not, thanks to that connection I got a new passport two days later. I didn't know who he was and wouldn't have dared approach him myself, but I was surely glad that Ma was able to step in and save the day. Without her, that mistake would have changed the course of history for me.

■ ■ ■

The USGA brought us all to New York the night before the voyage to Great Britain and hosted a special dinner for the team and some select USGA members at the Waldorf Astoria. My friend Jean Hopkins was traveling with us, since she had been picked as the reserve, and Mom and Dad had also come to see us off. It was all very exciting. Our team captain, Glenna Collett Vare, was the only one of us who had ever been to Europe. The next morning was a cold and rainy day, but that didn't stop a whole bunch of New Yorkers from showing up to see us off. We were sailing over on the

RMS Mauretania, a 56,000 ton, two-funneled cruise ship which just a year earlier had undergone a complete renovation.

After arriving at Southampton on the south coast of England, the team took the train to London where we stayed for a number of days. We knew we'd need to practice as soon as we arrived and would need to get our land legs back after a week on the ship. We were invited to play a few informal matches around London at such renowned courses as Sunningdale, The Berkshire, and Roehampton. We had to accustom ourselves to the British courses since it was our first time over there and we'd been told that the grass was shorter than ours, and the soil more sandy and soft. I'd also heard that the rough was rougher, because the tall grass was never cut, and the hazards really were hazardous. We knew the main thing that would bother us inland golfers was the coastal wind. As we learned, it's nearly always blowing and we needed to practice to allow for those air currents.

Enid Wilson, a three-time British Ladies champion and member of the first-ever Great Britain and Ireland Curtis Cup team, was an author and writer for the Daily Telegraph. *She was known as one of women's golf's contrarian free spirits and wrote, "The girls will be given transportation to and from the clubs which is no small item in view of the present petrol rationing situation in England."*

In between practice, we got to do a little bit of sightseeing. We were amazed to see all of the scaffolding holding up the buildings and learn about how much London was bombed during the war. I'll never forget the stench of burning and I began to realize what the British had gone through. I really had no concept. And neither did a lot of Americans who hadn't yet traveled there.

We read in the papers that the British golf writers were all up in arms that the British players were at a disadvantage because they'd been put through a grueling qualification trial in April, just four weeks before the matches. That left them with little time to practice and bond as a team. Conversely, our team had been announced by the USGA in January and that gave us the opportunity to compete and practice in warmer climates. The USGA had also arranged for us to practice with some of the smaller English golf balls. Because these matches were under the jurisdiction of the R&A Rules, the U.S. players had the choice to play either the large U.S. ball or the smaller English ball. I chose to play an English Slazenger ball, in both the Cup matches and the British the following week. To be honest, I wished I could have played with it in the States because of how it reacted in the wind and how I could chip and putt with it.

The drumbeat that the British team was not fully prepared continued before the matches had even begun. Enid Wilson took the Ladies Golf Union (LGU) to task for having accepted the USGA's invitation to restart the international matches too soon after a 10-year lapse (because of World War II). Writing in Golf Illustrated, *Wilson reported how the U.S. team, while from vastly different parts of the States, were competing with and against each other on a regular basis on the vibrant U.S. circuit. "The American team has gone off to the Florida circuit and for the next ten weeks they will be taking part in a series of competitions, buoyed by the very fact that they are on the team due to visit Britain. Meanwhile, our valiant twenty will pursue their jobs, and run their homes, and at week-ends find their way by bus, train, or taxi to their home course and play perhaps eighteen holes with their friends. By way of competitions, they have monthly medals, running bogeys, and smaller fry, quite useless tuning for international golf."*

Whether for those reasons or not, Ms. Wilson's prediction became a reality when the U.S. team prevailed by 6 ½ points to 2 ½ on Royal Birkdale's storied links. On the first day, Louise and Grace Lenczyk was the only foursome team to lose to the Brits. They went down 3 & 2 to Jacqueline Gordon and Jean Donald. Despite that loss, the eventual clincher for the Cup came down to Louise, who was dormie two down in her match against Irish legend Philomena Garvey. Philomena was the winner of 15 Irish national titles and Curtis Cupper seven times. Louise, suffering from

*On the second hole of Royal Birkdale on my way to gaining the winning half
point for the United States team. The bunkers weren't raked, which made it more
challenging. As I got ready for this shot, I saw this photographer standing in the
way. I thought, "If this guys fool enough to stand there he deserves to be hit."
Despite that, I tried to maneuver my shot to make sure that didn't happen.
Photo courtesy Colorsport-Provincial Press.*

*a severe attack of hay fever, rallied to win the 17th and 18th and get a half
point. That gave the U.S. the overall win. As a first-timer in the Curtis Cup,
Louise had never encountered a match finishing with a half point and was
headed for the 19th hole. Unaware that the match had ended, Louise got a
scolding from her captain Glenna Collett Vare for not shaking hands with
Philomena quickly enough.*

Enid Wilson wrote in **Golf Monthly** *under the headline "Charming
Ladies", "It would be impossible to have met a more charming or cheery
crowd than these American ladies and they have been exceedingly popular
with all who were fortunate enough to meet them and see them play. They
had a great advantage over our side, for to them the Curtis Cup Match was*

just another day's golf and, in comparison to our girls, they have a vast tournament experience. That alone would have decided the match in their favor."

■ ■ ■

"Georgia Girl is Queen of Golf. British Weather Bad; Louise's Golf Was Good." Front-page headline—Golf World, *June 9, 1948.*

The weather during the Curtis Cup hadn't been great, but we came to find out that it was just a drop in the bucket compared to what we would face when we got to Royal Lytham & St Annes Golf Club the following week for the British Ladies' Amateur.

The weather really turned out to be our toughest opponent; relentless wind, sometimes gusting 30 miles and hour, and rain driving sideways made it more of an endurance test—nothing like anything us Americans where used to. It was the kind of weather no one would even dream of competing in today. We'd rather have all been shuttered up in front of a fire. Thankfully, I had a knack for playing well in bad weather and, strangely enough, I liked wind in those days. I would go to Sea Island and practice in that kind of weather. I think it made me concentrate more and I didn't try to force the ball. I just tried to swing at it and make contact. I knew I couldn't beat the wind, so instead I let it help me. However, to this day, I've never experienced golf in weather like that. I don't remember ever being dry. It just rained and blew non-stop. During that whole week, I was the only player in the field of 109 to break par on the front nine. And I did it twice. Nobody broke par on the back nine—such were the treacherous conditions.

Some of the women in Britain still played in skirts. I couldn't imagine playing in those conditions dressed like that. Thank goodness Aunt Vera had been in the Red Cross and she gave me her wool uniform. If I hadn't had those slacks I don't know what I would have done. I also borrowed by brother Rell's long underwear, and one kind Englishwoman loaned me a pair of rain pants. I offered to buy them but she refused. Instead, said she would love to be able to buy my slacks at the end of the week. Of course, I didn't take her money either when I left her my slacks and a jacket before returning to the States.

For many reasons, I have to admit that if it hadn't been for my caddie Tish Rimmer, I wouldn't have been able to do what I did that week. Tish was a little English guy, probably in his 50's, and he became my caddie in the strangest of ways. And it began with the LGU. I showed up at Lytham expecting to carry by own bag and this little guy walked up with his cap on, like a typical British-looking caddie. He said, "Lassie, I'm going to caddie for you." He continued, "I normally caddie for Miss Stephens and some of us guys are unhappy about the way she's been treated by the LGU." Well, I was standing there wondering what he was leading up to. He went on, "All the caddies got together and decided that, as the U.S. National champion, we wanted to make sure you won next week. So we drew straws on who would caddie for you and I won." Well, that was Tish. And, let me tell you, those caddies were right. He ended up as my secret weapon that week.

Many of the women of the LGU later became my friends and I grew to have the utmost respect for them. But, they were having a tough go of it with the press that year. First, they were criticized about the lateness of the selection of the British & Irish Curtis Cup team. And then, they caused a significant controversy when they failed to name Frances "Bunty" Stevens to the team. There was a huge uproar as Bunty's father was a professional at one of the courses near Royal Birkdale. Bunty seemed to be a shoe-in for selection; she had been good enough to play for England before, and the previous three years had won practically all of her representative matches. When the team was announced at Birkdale, where she was a member, people were staggered by the snub. I don't know what the politics were behind that decision, but it really caused a stir.

Before things got going, Tish said, "The only thing I ask of you is, if the flag is over here but I say aim it over there—I mean for you to hit it there." Well, I'd never played that kind of golf. The tournament started and I quickly found out that he was right. When he said aim in a specific direction, he meant it and I learned to trust him. A lot of times I'd say something like, "I'd like a 6-iron," and he'd say. "I don't think so." And, mostly, he was right. I was a bump and run player because of Dad's course and, fortunately, that bump and run came in handy. It was even easier for me because I was playing the small English ball.

As we worked our way through the week toward the finals, I looked at that little guy and I really thought he might shrink in all that rain. On the last day, the weather was so bad we had to hire an extra person to carry the golf umbrella because he couldn't manage the bag and the umbrella, and neither could I. Every day, everything was sopping wet and so cold.

Unfortunately for Dot Kirby, my close friend and Curtis Cup teammate, we came up against each other in the quarterfinals. By that time, I had beaten Dot in the finals of all the 1947 women's amateur majors—the Southern Amateur, the Western Open, and the U.S. Amateur.

That week, Golf World *called Dot Kirby "The champion runner-up in the country. Consequently, she was a little more earnest about getting past Miss Suggs than usual; their close friendship was superseded by an extra desire to win, with practically no putts being conceded. Louise Suggs, after a 75-minute rest from defeating Dot Kirby, went out into the teeth of the storm to take on Dorothy Kielty—two Americans in one day! Louise was determined and silent and talked only to her jockey-sized caddy."*

I beat Dot and then Dorothy Kielty to get to the 36-hole final against Jean Donald. During the morning round against Jean, my

Royal Lytham in 1948. It was the kind of weather no one would even dream of competing in today. Associated Press photo.

best shot came on the 13ᵗʰ—a 235-yard, par-4. I had missed my drive badly and I was just out of the rough and 90 yards from the green. The rain was just pouring and the wind was sweeping right across the hole. Tish handed me a 7-iron and told me to aim at a narrow bunker at the right of the green. It was at least 20 yards to the right of the flag. He told me to hit it hard. By this time, I already knew to trust him and do exactly as he told me. So, I let fly and the ball started straight for the bunker, drifted rapidly to the left, landed on the green four yards in front of the flag, bounced twice, and went in for an eagle. Well, the British crowds were typically polite and a small group of Americans hooped a bit. I learned later that an Englishman was standing close to Jean and, as she addressed her pitch shot of 80 yards, he said, "Well, she has this for a half." She did make a good shot, using the same approach as me, and also nearly holed it. It missed by inches and trickled past the hole by a couple of feet. That put me one up and on the way to being three up by the time we went in for lunch.

As bad as the weather had been in the morning, it took a turn for the worse that afternoon. Gale-force winds blew in from the Irish Sea and the gallery dwindled to a hardy few. To give you an idea how bad the weather was, I shot 82 and 85, and Jean scored 85 and 83. That afternoon, Jean came back at me and got back to one down by the turn. I got it back to two at the 11th, but then I got myself all hung up in the rough for a string of three holes from the 13th through the 15th and found myself one down with three to play. I won the 16th to square the match and we halved the 17th to be all square going down the 36th hole of this marathon. It was there that my second went into a greenside bunker and I was able to explode out to six feet. Jean had missed the green right and chipped to 30 feet. So, it came down to the putts. She missed her first, leaving me with my six-footer to win, which I missed. She then missed her next putt, which gave me the win. Both of our putts were jittery on that last hole but my putt was less jittery than hers. I still remember standing on the 36th tee, the hole that would decide the championship, and I really didn't care at that point if I won or if I lost. I just wanted to get inside where it was warm.

■ ■ ■

It was a great week, full of many terrific memories. But there is one in particular that sticks with me. I've said many times that I've admired Bobby Jones for as long as I can remember. Well, that remained true even during the week of the British, when his storied history inadvertently stymied me during one of my matches. I drove near a bunker to the left on Lytham's 17th. Well, it just happened to be the exact spot from where Bobby Jones hit what some called the best golf shot in the history of the Open Championship. He was tied with Al Watrous on the final day of the 1926 Championship. On his second shot Bobby took a mashie from a hard sandy lie and hit it onto the green just inside his opponent's ball. He went on to win the first of his three Open Championship titles, and that shot has been credited with helping make that happen. To commemorate the shot, they put a bronze plaque near a bunker and that's right where my ball lay! I got out, but it was the only time in my life I wasn't pleased to see Bobby Jones' name in front of me.

Ultimately, I was so grateful to Tish for that win. I'll tell you, I would have loved for that guy to caddie for me all the time. We stayed friends and kept in touch from time to time through letters. I also remained good friends with Jean Donald. She came to the U.S. in 1950 to play in the Curtis Cup and the U.S. Amateur. By then, I was professional and had signed with MacGregor. I went to Buffalo to watch the matches and then drove with a few of the British girls: Jean, Jesse Valentine, and Jean Bisgood, to Atlanta, where the Amateur was being played at Eastlake Country Club. On the way down, we stopped in Cincinnati to show them through the MacGregor plant. They were truly amazed at the magnitude of the facility.

Jean lived on the east coast of Scotland at Gullane, near St. Andrews. Her house was right on the first tee. She always said to me that Gullane was the prettiest golf course in the prettiest area of the country. Well, I said to her that I'd love to come over and play it with her. I never made it over before she passed away, but I did play it by myself in her memory. And she was correct. It is the prettiest course that I've ever seen in that area.

I found out, after the fact, that the hotel waiters had a bet amongst themselves around the championship and that whoever won had to buy me a steak dinner. Well, this nice-looking young man came up and said, "Miss Suggs, I won and I am to buy you dinner." So, he served me my dinner and he asked if I wanted a cocktail. Well, I'd had sips of whiskey at the house with Mom and Dad but I'd never had a cocktail before. So, naively, I said, "Yes, I'd like a martini." In those days in Britain, they made martinis with half vermouth and half gin. It turned out to be the worst tasting thing I'd ever had. But I must say it did warm me up after being so cold. It was also the best steak I'd ever had, probably because I was so hungry and tired. When we got on the train to return to London that night, the misery continued as the heat wasn't working. I ended up sleeping in my clothes and overcoat and anything else I could find to pile on top of me. I think back on how frigid it was that whole week. I was so cold, my teeth were actually chattering. You cannot believe how frozen I was. My knuckles actually cracked on the ship coming back from being so cold and wet for that long.

When we left the British Isles, the American gals left all of the possessions that we didn't absolutely have to have, because the British didn't have anything because of the War. We gave them clothes, shoes, and even left our golf clubs with them. Except for me. I couldn't leave my clubs because I had to play an exhibition for Gulf in Pittsburgh as soon as I got back.

When we returned to New York, the Mauretania docked at about 10 p.m. but it took us until 2 a.m. to get through customs. They even unpacked the trophy and looked inside it. I was told that when fellow Atlantan Charlie Yates won the British title in 1938, customs unpacked the trophy and found it stuffed with his dirty laundry.

■ ■ ■

That win just popped the cork out of the bottle for me. I had gone as far as I could go as an amateur. As I sailed back, the manufacturers were waiting for me on the jetty to try to sign me as a professional. In the actual moment of winning, all I felt was relief that I'd be off the golf course. When I got back on the ship, I thought, "Well that's it. I don't have anything else to win as an amateur." And I really didn't.

Time to Join the Professionals

With the exception of my first Georgia title, I won all of my major amateur titles while I was working for Gulf Oil. At the time I was selected for the Curtis Cup team in 1948, Gulf was the sponsor of the national radio show, "We the People." The show invited Dad and me to be interviewed alongside Grantland Rice before I headed over to Great Britain, which we gladly did. A few weeks later, when I was sailing home to the U.S. after I won the British Ladies' Amateur Championship, I got a shore to ship call from the Gulf Oil folks. They were excited about my win and said that the show wanted to do a follow-up interview with Grantland and me in New York City as soon as I got back. This was around the time the show was being transferred from radio to television. In fact, it was the first nationally televised show of that type in the country. During my segment, they wanted me to hit a cotton ball in the studio. Back then, the mic's were stationary and didn't move. "If I swing this club it's going to hit that mic," I said. "Just try with a practice swing," they replied. Unfortunately for them I was proven right. I hit that mic and just about blew out their ears.

After that interview, Gulf arranged for me to play an exhibition at the Fox Chapel Club in Pittsburgh. Mom and Dad had come to New York to meet me when my ship arrived and, after the "We the People" interview, Dad went back to Georgia while Mom stayed to accompany me to Pittsburgh. While we were still in New York, I received a phone call and a man's voice said, "Miss Suggs. This is the pilot for Gulf Oil—where do you want the plane?" "Well, at the airport, of course!" I replied, all the while thinking, "dumb cracker." He patiently asked, "Which one?" I laughed to myself, "Now, who is the dumb cracker?" Shows what I knew—I didn't realize there was more than one New York City airport. Chagrinned, I said, "Tell me where you'll be and I'll find you."

We flew from New York to Pittsburgh on a DC3, the biggest plane in the sky in those days. While I had flown a little bit, this was Mom's first time on a plane—a big moment for her. When we arrived, we were greeted by Mr. C.M. Gile, the vice president of Gulf, and were taken to the roof of the Gulf building in Pittsburgh for a promotional photo shoot. I was told to hit a golf ball from the edge of the 20-story building right into what's known as "The Point"— where the Allegheny River joins with the Monongahela to form the Ohio River. I couldn't believe it. I had no idea this was the plan and was wearing a skirt and high heels. I kid you not, had there been a good gust of wind, I'd have gone right over the edge with the ball! I was dumb enough to do it but the photographer was dumber than I was—he was on a ladder above me.

When all was said and done, I thought, "These are things that just don't happen to a Georgia girl like me." There I was, hanging with one of the heads of the company I worked for, after they sent the company plane just for me. It was somewhat over-whelming. There were a few occasions when I felt completely out of my element around some of the executives. Dad had acquired a level of comfort around people like that because of his baseball career, and he used to tell me to just be myself. But a DC3—being sent just for me to do a photo shoot? Cheese and crackers! Some of my work colleagues back in the office in Atlanta used to tease the heck out of me for it.

Around this time, there were all kinds of rumors in the press about the possibility of me turning professional. I had been with Gulf for eight years, and after the Pittsburgh exhibition Mr. Gile said to me, "Louise, you've done so much for us and I guarantee you will always have a job. But, you've gone as far as you can in the company." In those days, women weren't put in managerial

One good gust of wind and I would have been in the Allegheny too.
You can see someone's foot steadying the bench.

positions. I was at the top of the pay scale for a woman and even that wasn't a whole heck of an amount of money. But it was a lot to me. I was still living at home paying rent to my parents. I really enjoyed my job and, despite what Mr. Gile said to me, if I hadn't gone on to play golf professionally, I still think I might have done well in the business world. Shortly after I left the company, they promoted a woman named Patty to be the comptroller of Gulf Oil in Pittsburgh. She was the friend of a good pal of mine from Cleveland. I saw myself in Patty to certain extent, and I thought to myself, "Well if she can head up a department, then so could I." It was really a moot point, because the next chapter of my golf career was about to begin.

Flying in the company plane.

When I got back from England, the buzz about me turning professional was at its height. The pinnacle of women's amateur golf at the time was winning either the U.S. Amateur or the British Ladies Amateur. And I had won them both. I figured, "Why press my luck? Move on while you're ahead." By this point, each of the big three equipment manufacturers was trying to get to me to turn professional and sign with them. Wilson, Spalding, and MacGregor were all making overtures. I knew for certain that I didn't want to go where Patty Berg and Babe Zaharias were and, since they were with Wilson, that company was out of consideration. Between the other two, it was Dad who tipped the scales towards MacGregor. I knew his career in professional sports had given him the experience to know what he was talking about. He told me that MacGregor was a good deal and that we wouldn't do any better. Not only would I be their first woman and, therefore, the senior one going forward, the money they offered was eye-popping. I got $25 a day for expenses, the use of a car, $500 bonuses with wins, plus royalties from clubs sold with my name on them. Back then you could stay in a motel for $5 a night and buy a steak for $2 so, for me, it was a lot of money. Dad and I were in a meeting room finalizing the deal with Hugo Goldsmith, chairman of MacGregor, when Dad surprised all of us by saying, "Mr. Goldsmith, I think you probably want to do the right thing. Don't you think Louise deserves a bonus for signing with you?" I was a little taken aback. I would have been scared to even bring that up, but, by golly, they agreed to give me $5,000. It was a heck of a deal.

Once the contract terms were set, I knew I had to let Gulf know I was leaving. Walter Etzel had retired by then and Jack Russell was my boss. I went in, burst into tears, and said, "I don't want to leave Gulf." To which he said, "Don't be a fool. If we could give you that kind of money we would. But we can't. You have to do this."

I also thought that it would be proper to call Joe Dey, executive director of the USGA, to ask if it was okay to turn pro. He was somewhat startled that I called, and he gave not only his consent but also his best wishes. I shared with him that my goal was to help with the development of women's golf, and that I felt I could best do that with MacGregor.

After the deal was signed and sealed, I went to MacGregor's headquarters in Cincinnati to get acquainted with the company. Tony Penna was the head golf designer and, since they didn't have the equipment set up for me yet, he arranged a handmade set of clubs. They had to make them quickly because I had an upcoming exhibition with Bobby Jones at Highlands Country Club in North Carolina. After meeting with Tony, Henry Cowen, president of the company (and a man I liked and respected), said, "Come with me."

Signing the contract. From left: Dad, me, and MacGregor President Henry Cowen.
Photo courtesy Golf Digest Resource Center.

We walked out in the parking lot and there was a brand new 98 Oldsmobile convertible. I thought, "That's mine?" Boy, I thought I was hot stuff. And it dawned on me in that moment that I was actually being paid to play golf. It boggled my mind.

Charles Curtis, executive sports editor and golf writer for the Los Angeles Times *reported, "Louise Suggs is a physical oddity in women's golf. In a sport pretty well dominated by big husky women, Louise is an unusual person. Not only is she slender but her arms and wrists are extremely small. Yet she hits the ball as far as any woman golfer."*

The company began sending me out to give exhibitions and clinics at clubs all across the country. They had my schedule laid out for me; hotels, the people I was to meet, etc., but I was by myself and had to find my own way to those places. Don't get me wrong,

I was all gung-ho and thought this was the way it was supposed to be—loading and unloading the car, keeping my shoes shined, the whole kaboodle. I crisscrossed the country, travelling 16,000 miles and doing one stretch of 28 exhibitions in 28 days. They trusted me enough to send me out by myself to represent the company—and apparently I got the job done.

Alex J. Morrison, a California golf pro and renowned instructor, observed one of Louise's clinics and said, "I was impressed with her sweetness and modesty, and also her marked willingness to do anything within her power to help other golfers improve their games. She demonstrated that she can play a bigger variety of shots than other feminine champions have shown to date. Even the ball comes under the spell of her charm."

When I look back and compare to how things are today, MacGregor and the other two leading manufacturers really used women quite a bit in their advertising. My public exposure was right up there with Hogan, Nelson, Armour, and Demaret. I was once featured beside them in an ad with the headline, "MacGregor golf clubs and balls excel in action. The record of the greatest names in golf proves it." I also appeared in numerous single page ads by myself which, to be frank, is not something you see today's golf companies doing with women.

When it came to equipment, Tony Penna would often ask me a lot of questions about the best clubs for women and I would share my two bits. I didn't do any design work and wouldn't have known how to grind a ferrule or anything, but I did spend some time in the factory where I got to know many of the supervisors in different areas of production. Of course there were no women around so the language left a bit to be desired. Whenever I came in, whoever saw me first would yell, "Dame on the floor," or, "Gal on the floor. Clean it up boys!"

Until Tony joined MacGregor as head designer, golf clubs didn't change much from year to year. In that regard, he was a really talented guy and a pretty good player as well. Some time in the early 1950's, I played as Tony's partner in a couple of tournaments. He was a small man, not too much taller than me, but despite his size he hit the ball a ton. We played an event in the Orlando Open at Dubsdread Golf Course. It was a mixed selective drive alternate shot format and he always said, "Now Louise, you just hit it on the golf course and I'll knock the heck out of it." That day he was hitting it fairly straight, so I was hitting the second shot most of the time with his ball. For some reason, I was knocking it stiff on pretty much every shot. In turn, he must have missed five putts from within five feet. He had that reputation. It was pretty well known that even if Tony made a short putt it was an accident. When we got to the 10th, which was a dogleg left par-4, I hit my drive into a good position, which left him with the chance to go for it on his drive. And he did. He cut the corner and made it, which left me with only a nine-iron to the green. Well, I hit that thing straight into the hole. Before he could say a word, I turned to him and said, "There. I'm sick and tired of you missing those putts." He got a big kick out of that.

For many years, MacGregor specialized in custom-made clubs. The company didn't make women's clubs when I signed with them and they had to retool the factory to get into the market. Because of that, they took out a $5 million insurance policy on me to protect their start-up costs. One day, Mr. Cowen called me to his office and told me they had broken even on their investment in women's clubs and had, therefore, cancelled the insurance policy. At that time, they were making most of their money in women's clubs in Japan. The smaller men started playing with Suggs clubs because they found that the shorter clubs suited them better—and they bought them by the ton. Mr. Cowen told me, "Louise, we are going to take your name off the clubs we're selling in Japan because more men will buy them. It will be the same club so we will still pay you the royalties." It seemed a fair thing for them to do because, in a sense, I had put them in business in that part of the world. They honored the deal. I'm proud to say that, for a while, the Suggs club was the most popular woman's club on the market.

It wasn't just Japanese men who played with my clubs. One time, my dear friend Davis Love III introduced Paul Azinger, PGA Tour star and 2008 Ryder Cup captain, to me on Sea Island. The first thing out of his mouth was, "My first set of clubs was a Louise Suggs set of clubs." Then he said, "Nice to meet you."

■ ■ ■

Thanks to Mr. Cowen, my corporate relationships during my competitive days expanded beyond MacGregor. He introduced me to David Smith, founder of David Smith Sportswear, and helped me sign a contract with the company. They made Lynbrook dresses and they wanted me to help promote their expansion into golf dresses. I told David that they'd never be successful in golf unless they designed separates. They went ahead and made their Lynbrook dress—labeled "Louise Suggs by Lynbrook." However, they later took my advice and introduced a pretty successful line of separates called "Golf-A-Rounds by Louise Suggs."

The David Smith relationship was fun for me because I always had an affinity for clothes. I didn't have a large wardrobe, but I really enjoyed good clothes. One of my style trademarks on Tour was my headwear. I always tried to be different. One of my favorites was what I called my legionnaire's cap. It's now called a painter's cap. After I started wearing them, Patty Berg and Babe started sporting them too—so I quit wearing them.

I can't say that I approve of what the girls play in nowadays. However, the skirts we had to play in during our era were not fun and they really restricted your swing. If you got on a side hill lie and the wind was blowing—man-oh-man, you could just sail away. I later wore slacks or Bermuda shorts with knee socks. I

One of my style trademarks on tour was my headwear. I bought this hat for
$1.98 in the basement of Davidson's in Atlanta. I wore it for the first time when
I won the Southern Amateur, so it became somewhat of a good luck charm.
It's now displayed in the World Golf Hall of Fame.

first remember wearing shorts on a golf course in 1954. We were playing the Western Open at Glen Flora Country Club in North Chicago, where I lost to Betty Jameson 6 & 5 in the final. In an earlier round, it had stormed so badly that they called us in. We got into the locker room and changed out of our soaked clothes and put them away. Between five thirty and six o'clock, all of a sudden we got the message that we were going back on the course. By that time, we were all dressed in shorts because we were going to a BBQ that night. We said we couldn't put our wet clothes back on so the Women's Western Association made an exception and let us play in shorts.

In the ensuing years, the rules began to loosen and we didn't have to wear skirts all the time. However, the USGA remained kind of sticky. In 1957, we showed up at Winged Foot for the U.S. Women's Open dressed mostly in Bermuda shorts and knee socks, and they wouldn't let us in the clubhouse. We all had to go out and buy skirts. Compared to what they wear today, it's hard to imagine that the length of the Bermuda shorts we wore wasn't acceptable. And now I suppose I've become that generation of folks who don't like today's fashions. And so it goes.

Starting a New Industry for Women—the LPGA

Things couldn't have been more different for women's golf in the late 1940's and early 1950's than they are today. All in all, those of us involved in trying to get a tour together were a pretty gutsy bunch. It didn't even occur to us that we couldn't succeed. We survived in spite of ourselves.

The seeding of women's professional golf began in earnest after the Second World War. The major golf manufacturers started to realize that the next big thing in the industry would be the women's market and they began signing women golfers to represent them. Of the big three golf manufacturing companies at that time, Wilson had Patty Berg, Babe, and Betsy Rawls, while Spalding had the Bauer sisters (Marlene and Alice) and Betty Jameson. MacGregor didn't have any women. That's why Dad suggested that I sign with them.

The companies sent us around the country, to small towns mostly, to help drum up both awareness and business for the women's game. My task was to team with the company's local sales reps for exhibitions and clinics. When I joined MacGregor, the company had Byron Nelson, Ben Hogan, and Jimmy Demaret as their big names. They asked Byron if he'd take me along on his exhibition route and train me on how to conduct clinics. He agreed and I traveled with him and his wife, Louise, in a limousine all over the Midwest for about six weeks. Byron jokingly warned that he was going to put me to the test and did so at one clinic when, out of the blue, he said, "I'm going to have Louise work with me today and the first thing she's going to do is show you how to hit a 2-iron." Well, everyone knows how hard it is to hit a 2-iron, particularly on the spot like that. Thankfully, I was pretty good with my long irons and I did okay. Baptism by fire, you might say.

It was around this time that Hope Seignious (of Greensboro, North Carolina) was tournament manager for what was then the Women's Professional Golfers' Association. Along with some other visionary women like Betty Hicks, Hope did a great job of putting together a smattering of open tournaments around the country where professionals could play alongside a field of amateurs. It was not easy going, and the WPGA ultimately didn't last. It was Hope who helped get a national open up and running in Spokane, Washington from 1946 through 1948. Many said, had it not been for her, it would have taken many more years before women had a national open. As we began to form what would become the LPGA, we took over running the Open from 1949 through 1952, and the USGA assumed responsibility for it from 1953 onwards.

I kept running into many of the gals signed with the other companies as we all traveled across the country conducting clinics and exhibitions. Eventually someone suggested, "Since we're out here doing this anyway, why don't we find someone to put up some money and we'll play for it as we go around?" We knew that the PGA, which was well established by that time, was requiring more and more money to put on tournaments for the men in certain cities. In some cases, a prize fund of say $10,000 wasn't balancing against the income coming in at the gate. We realized this was an opportunity for us as we were confident that top women's golf could draw a crowd to justify the purse money; as evidenced by what happened at the Capital City Club in 1948 when Dot Kirby and I put on an exhibition match against Babe and Patty Berg. We filled the gate.

With this concept in mind, we began to string some tournaments together—financed mostly by various civic clubs like the Civitan Club, Lions Club, or Kiwanis Club. We asked them to put up the prize money, charge spectator fees, and get folks to play in a pro-am type event alongside us for two or three days. We'd then play on the final day with each other. Our scores counted for every round, including those with the amateurs, and if any funds remained after the prize money was given out, it went to a local charity. There weren't any major companies lining up to sponsor us at first, but our civic approach ended up helping us with corporate America. Many of the civic club members were executives with big companies and later became eager to be involved.

In 1949, there were only about seven tournaments scattered around the country in which women professionals could compete: two Florida tournaments, the Western Open, National Open, Tam O'Shanter, Texas Open, and the Harbscrabble Invitational. It was around this time that we began to talk about bringing Fred Corcoran on board to help get us more events. Fred had done that job for the men from 1937 to 1947, before being hired by Wilson to help the company promote women on their professional tour staff. But the real visionary for all of this was L.B. Icely, the head of Wilson at the time. I always believed that he was really forward thinking in his view of the women's game. In May 1949, during the Eastern Open in Essex Falls, New Jersey, a group of us met and agreed to bring Fred on board—his salary jointly funded by Wilson, MacGregor, and Spalding. The Ladies Professional Golf Association formally incorporated the following year in 1950.

Fred got quite a bit going for us and things began to move along nicely with the big three manufacturers supporting both the PGA and the LPGA. At some point, however, the powers that be in those companies decided that the PGA was established enough and didn't need more help. So they withdrew their funding. Unfortunately, because they were pulling out of the men's tour, they felt that they couldn't support the LPGA either and stopped funding us as well. We were just getting going and we really needed that money, and it fell back to us players to beat the bushes and find our own sponsors. So, a group of us began going to numerous lunches and meetings to drum up support. I never ate so much rubber chicken in my life.

As a woman, it wasn't at all easy going into some of those corporate offices trying to sell a women's golf tournament. I was insulted and called a lot of things you'd never want to hear, but I just gritted my teeth because I knew what our end goal was. In those days, a lot of men didn't like or respect female athletes. However, there was a special group of men who really went out of their way to pitch in. Helen Lengfeld introduced some of the key ones to us. Helen was a California businesswoman and editor of *The Golfer* magazine, and really worked her connections on our behalf. She got us a tournament at Pebble Beach for five years running and introduced us to Alvin Handmacher, a New Yorker who turned the $500,000 Weathervane women's clothing business into a $6 million empire. He sponsored a series of tournaments in various states, with bonus prizes based on a player's cumulative performance. Helen also connected us with Jack McCauliffe of the Triangle Conduit and Cable Company. His company sponsored the Triangle Round Robin series of tournaments, which I won three times. Helen didn't get enough credit for what she did for the LPGA. However, after the LPGA incorporated, we elected Helen chairman of the LPGA Sponsor's Advisory Committee and gave her a vote of appreciation for all the work she did for women's golf throughout the country.

Despite the fact that things were beginning to move along for our fledgling tour, the finances for our tournaments were never steady. One time, I was on the 17th tee at an event in Oklahoma when someone ran out to let me know that the tournament organizer had run off with the entire prize fund. I went on to win that tournament by four shots but not one of us made a dime. You'd think we'd have been down in the dumps, because it's not like money was flowing freely for any of us, but we all ended up sitting in the clubhouse singing, joking, and just carrying on like everything was just fine. And in a way, it really was.

We reached a point in 1958 when our tour was really struggling and, in yet another attempt to get help, I called up Harold Sargent. He was a friend of mine, the head professional at Eastlake Golf Club in Atlanta, and the president of the PGA. I asked if he could help set up a meeting for us with the PGA at The Masters, to which he agreed. I then called Bobby Jones and asked if he could arrange for us to buy three clubhouse tickets, and he was kind enough to send us complimentary passes. So off we went—Marilynn Smith, Mary Lena Faulk, and I. The goal was to get the PGA to help us but not necessarily join with us. At that time, Ed Carter was in charge of booking the PGA tournaments and during the meeting, it was agreed that if Ed went into a town and couldn't get a tournament booked for the men, he would try and get it for the women instead. The arrangement worked pretty well as Ed secured a few tournaments for us.

"When Louise was president of the organization, we were at a tournament where I happened to have a room next door to hers, and every night I would be awakened at around midnight by a noise coming from Louise's room. Turns out it was a typewriter. Louise was writing letters to sponsors trying to get us tournaments. Each night she worked past midnight and then she'd go out and play the next day. I never could figure out how she could do all of that and still play so well. People don't realize how much those women worked to make the tour possible."—Mickey Wright; World Golf Hall of Fame member, winner of 82 LPGA titles, and the only woman to have held all four major titles at the same time.

■ ■ ■

We really began the LPGA as a ragtag bunch with all manner of different swings and personalities. It was entertaining, to say the least, but there was often some tension. Imagine a bunch of strong-willed, competitive women traveling together, competing against each other, and then having to practically live together because everywhere we played was a small town. Someone once asked me if Babe Zaharias, Patty Berg, and I got together at the beginning of the week to decide who'd win that week's tournament. The answer was easy. "Have you ever seen three cats fight over a plate of fish?"

From left: Patty Berg, Babe Zaharias, and I playfully wrestle for the World Championship Golf Tournament trophy at Tam O'Shanter.
Photo Bettman/Corbis/AP Images.

I suppose it really shouldn't come as a surprise that our generation produced a tough bunch of women. During the war, men had to go into service and the women were left to do a lot of the heavy lifting. Working for Gulf, I oversaw a lot of Atlanta's city service stations and it was the women who pumped gas, cleaned cars, changed tires and oil, and so forth. I really believe that those experiences helped develop the kind of attitude that helped the LPGA get going. We were the kind of people that if someone said, "You can't do that," by golly we were going to prove you wrong and do it. And we did!

In addition to competing each week, we had no choice but to do a lot of the work at the tournaments ourselves. We literally ran the tour out of the trunks of our cars. Once we found out that Betty Hicks was as smart as a whip and could type we said, "Okay, you're the secretary." Then we'd assign other players to oversee the scorecards, make the pairings, write the checks, and call the press at the end of the day to report the scores. Betty often drove to the next tournament with our homemade scoreboard strapped to the top of her car.

The usual drill when we got to tournament sites, often after driving all night, was to train the marshals and show the grounds crew how we wanted the course marked. If we weren't pounding the stakes ourselves, which wasn't uncommon, we pretty much did everything; even grabbing a trowel now and then to cut our own holes. But sometimes we didn't have any control over how the courses were manicured. It's hard to believe, but we'd play courses where you couldn't tell the difference between the fairway and the rough. There were a couple of times we had to bring in farm equipment to help define the difference. If we had bad weather and we had to lift and place, knowing where the fairway ended and the rough started was sometimes tough. Course conditions were often so bad we had to have local rules as to where players were allowed to pull weeds on the greens that might be in their line.

We played our courses fairly long because the local male club members didn't want us to shoot lights out. We basically played courses from the men's tees; playing 6700 or 6800-yard tracks. If you shot a 70 you had really played a good round of golf. Hitting a 5-iron into a par four was almost unheard of and, more often than not, we were hitting 3-woods for our second shots. It makes me pause when I see LPGA players today hitting 7-irons 165 yards. I'd give a pretty penny to see them play with the equipment we used and with the course conditions we experienced.

We didn't have a whole bunch of players to begin with but the ones we had were good. I believe there were more shot makers than there are today; you had to learn to play the ball differently, not just because of the equipment but also because the golf courses weren't manicured like they are now. You might be playing on slow greens one week and then the next they'd be like greased lightning and you then had to acclimate yourself to that.

■ ■ ■

We were really like a tight-knit traveling circus. We practically lived out of our cars as we traversed the country from town to town and, because of that, we traveled in caravans for safety. There were times when we had to sleep in our cars and others where we'd have to drive all night and tee it up the next morning without a wink of sleep. You wouldn't believe the potholed roads we had to drive on—and that was if the roads were paved. I became an expert at fixing flats. Even buses didn't go to some of the towns we played in and luxury for us meant something as simple as finding a motel with a hot plate.

Marlene Bauer Hagge, a fellow Founder of the LPGA, was only 13 when she went on tour with her folks and her sister Alice (also an LPGA Founder). You could hand that little gal an electric frying pan and she could cook a meal better than you'd get in a gourmet restaurant. Because of her age, I found myself looking out for Marlene quite a bit and we ultimately became lifelong friends. She was very glamorous and I used to tease her that her pants were often so tight that if she had a dime in her pocket I'd be able to tell if it was heads or tails. We both still laugh about it to this day.

Sometimes, en route to the next town, our caravan would pull over in a nearby cornfield and there we'd cook dinner, sing songs, and settle in to sleep for the night. There was one time, somewhere in Oklahoma, where we hit a dead end on the road we were travelling and weren't sure which way to go. We were a little bit concerned until we realized that we were right beside a liquor store. Guess what happened next? We made a few purchases and made the best of a bad situation by enjoying ourselves all night until daylight broke and we could make our way back on to the proper route.

I got to where I could pack my car like an engineer. I had plenty of practice. In one year I traversed the country four times from coast to coast and put over 40,000 miles on my car. Whether it was evening clothes, golf clothes, rain gear, shoes, or a coffee pot—I could fit it all and I always packed it the same way. Every piece of my belongings was assigned to a specific part of the car. By the late 1950's, I carried a pretty heavy wardrobe: something like 18 pairs of shorts and pants, a couple dozen shirts, a dozen pair of shoes, miscellaneous sweaters and dress suits, and about 44 pounds of equipment. Thankfully, I always had a big car because there was no way I could have done it in some of today's teeny cars.

We pretty much had to do our own laundry because you just couldn't trust the motels to do it right. They would either ruin your clothes or, worse, steal them. So I got to where I'd wash my own clothes in the bathtub at night and just find anywhere I could hang them to dry. That included putting them in the back of the car with the windows down so that they'd dry on the way to the next town.

It was not an easy life, with all of the traveling and the packing and unpacking, but there were plenty of great times and fond memories. We would tease each other pretty hard but it was all in good fun and we ultimately had each other's backs. Don't get me wrong though, when it came to competition we wanted to beat each other like the best of them. When all was said and done, we'd take care of business together, write the checks, and move on. We'd have sing-a-longs in the clubhouse because there were quite a few good singers and musicians among us. A lot of folks may not know that Babe had a beautiful voice and could play the harmonica. And, when she wasn't being so cocky, she could even be quite funny.

I'll admit, if it hadn't been for Babe's zest for attention we might not have gotten the early support we did. She was a heck of an athlete and really knew how to play to the gallery. There is no question she was a character and often the crowd favorite. But the beginning of the LPGA might have been smoother going without her. A lot of my time as president in the late 1950's was spent trying to stop her from screwing things up since she really only cared about herself and not the rest of the tour. Her public reputation was in contrast to how some of us in close circles felt.

Because we were considered the top players, Babe, Patty Berg, and I were invited to participate in numerous entertainment endeavors. In 1950, I was asked to join Babe and Patty to star alongside Bob Hope and Bing Crosby in a 22-minute color motion picture called "Honor Caddie." It was a promotional short produced by the Western Golf Association to raise funds and awareness for the Evans Scholarship Fund. The whole thing was inspired by Chick Evans, the first amateur to win both the U.S. Amateur Championship and the U.S. Open in the same year. I knew Chick well from playing in the North & South at Pinehurst. He had started in golf as a caddie, like other golf greats Walter Hagen and Gene Sarazen, and because of his own experience, Chick wanted to start a scholarship fund to help other young boys and girls get into golf through caddying.

The producers flew Babe, Patty, and me to Hollywood and rented us a three-bedroom, three-bathroom apartment right on Sunset Boulevard. It was a pretty nice space and included a kitchen.

This particular week almost became the scene of yet another fire in my life—this one courtesy of Babe. We were there for 10 days during some really horrible weather. It was so cold that the production crew had an extra person hired just to carry our overcoats. We'd whip them off to make the shots, get major goose bumps in the 40-degree and windy weather, and then quickly put the coats back on. One night, after being out all day, the three of us were poop tired after working in the cold for so long. Babe said, "Let's order something in," which Patty and I thought was a fine idea. The food was delivered and Babe just stuck it in the oven and turned the heat on. Back then, takeout didn't come in Styrofoam but in cardboard boxes. In no time, our meal was smoldering and before long I could smell something burning. It dawned on me what was happening and I was able to get a wet towel and throw it on the smoking boxes to save what turned out to be a charred chicken dinner.

All in all it was a good week. Between Bing Crosby singing "Tomorrow Is My Lucky Day," Bob Hope's comedy, and our golf shots, the piece ended up being pretty good. It was distributed to clubs all over the country and used as the centerpiece at fund-raising events for the Evans program. Even today, the Evans Scholarship Fund is still a tremendous program.

■　■　■

The collective responsibilities of running our own tour went well beyond the preparation and wrap work. It extended to competitive play because we didn't have tournament officials. We had to do our own rulings. While it was a good thing that I used to know the Rules of Golf backwards and forwards, there was a personal downside because I'd frequently get called on to help with someone else's ruling when I was right in the middle of my own round. This was even more the case during my three years as president of the LPGA (between 1955 and 1957), because whoever was president was the boss, so to speak. There were numerous weird rules moments, which meant that I was constantly on the phone with the USGA, on my own dime, to make certain I was making the right decisions. I practically supported the phone company. Here I was, trying to play my own game and getting all hot and bothered about someone else's ruling. But that's how it was. We all had to do it.

For example, one year I was playing in St Louis, behind Betty Bush. I watched her hit a shot on a par three that got hung up in a tree. Her husband Eddie began tossing up a seat cane to try and dislodge it. When that didn't work, Betty saw a worker on the course and, still believing that she was supposed to identify the ball, was going to send him back to the barn to get a ladder. Well the Rules don't allow that. I had to yell, "Betty, unless you can identify it, it's lost. So come back and hit another one." Of course, they weren't intentionally trying to skirt the Rules, but they just didn't know. That was the case with a lot of the players. It kept those of us who were more familiar with the Rules pretty busy.

Bev Hanson and I both represented MacGregor and, because of that, our bags were identical. That led to an unfortunate moment when we were paired together in one particular tournament. Before we teed off, our bags had been side-by-side on the driving range and, while we were practicing, the caddies mistakenly mixed up the clubs. We didn't realize until the second hole, when I asked my caddie for a 2-iron. "Your 2-iron is not in here," he said. Bev looked in her bag and said, "I've got two 2-irons." We had to go through the whole mess of having to wait until after the round to make a phone call to the USGA to find out what to do. As it turned out, there wasn't a penalty because the mistake had not been deliberate. In the meantime, however, we couldn't make the pairings for the next day because the scores weren't final until we'd resolved the issue. That particular Rule has since been changed. That mistake would now be a two-stroke penalty per hole to a maximum of four.

Without question, the most heartbreaking Rules moment I recall being involved in happened at the 1957 U.S. Women's Open at Winged Foot. Jackie Pung shot a final round of 72 to finish the championship in the lead by a single shot from Betsy Rawls. Unfortunately, Jackie and her playing partner Betty Jameson had each taken a six on the fourth hole, but mistakenly both wrote five on the scorecard and signed it as such. The total of 72 written at the bottom of the card was Jackie's correct total score but because the box for the fourth hole showed a five instead of a six, Jackie technically had signed for a wrong score—the right total, but the wrong hole-by-hole. We went into a private room and went back and forth discussing the outcome with Joe Dey, executive director of the USGA, and Dick Tufts from Pinehurst, who was then president of the USGA. Sadly, there could only be one outcome—disqualification. Poor Dick was just overwhelmed by the fact that Jackie had actually won the championship by reporting the correct total but the score was just marked too low on one hole. I'm not sure I've ever seen a man that upset. I'm pretty certain it wouldn't have happened if the scoring area had been roped off like they do today. The press and spectators were all over Jackie as she was signing her card. There's no question in my mind that all the commotion and excitement prevented her from properly checking the card. Everyone, including the USGA folks, felt so awful that a collection was taken up for Jackie. She was given over $2,000—more than Betsy Rawls got as the eventual champion. However, it goes without saying that Jackie would have rather had the title than the money.

A Hall of Fame Career Gets into Full Swing

"No golfing attraction could be better than that produced at Palma Ceia."—Golf World, *January 1949*

I made my debut as a professional at the 1949 Tampa Open at Palma Ceia Golf and Country Club as one of only six professionals in the field. It was the first time that Babe and I had played in the same event as professionals and it was our first meeting in a 72-hole stroke play event. Because of that, the media had headlined the match-up between us as one of the big sports moments of that time. Naturally, I wanted to make sure I was prepared for the big occasion and so I took to the practice range as often as I could. Unfortunately, the preparation took its toll. After two practice rounds of 74, I ended up with a raw blister the size of a half-dollar on the heel of my right hand. It wasn't helped by the fact that I had never worn a golf glove. I didn't throughout my whole career. I had been hitting the ball well and really didn't want to make a big deal of the blister. However, some friends visiting from Atlanta noticed it when I grimaced when they shook my hand. I decided that, instead of another whole practice round the day before the tournament, I would give my hand a break by just practicing with three or four balls on a few of the more troublesome holes.

Louise went on to open with a round of 74 to share the lead with Peggy Kirk and Marjorie Lindsay. However, the grand head-to-head between Babe and Louise, hyped up by a hopeful media corps, was not to be. Patty Berg proved to be the spoiler by beating them both. Louise finished third. The Atlanta Journal *quoted Babe; "'She's a grand little player, and a great asset to the professional game,' said the big, bad, brawny Babe Zaharias."* Golf World *wrote, "Miss Berg, because of an automobile accident some years ago, which slowed her down, was not thought to be up to the Babe and Louise over the 72-hole medal play route. But she was, and thus a competent Triangle has been established in women's pro golf at the start of the 1949 season."*

■ ■ ■

In June 1949, Oklahoma City was the scene of the 20th anniversary of the Women's Western Open Championship, a major championship and the premier match play event in women's golf at that time. The field featured a star-studded combination of amateurs and professionals. Louise swept through them all to score her first professional title. She disposed of Patty Berg in the semis and Betty Jameson in the final, and joined Patty Berg and Babe as the only three-time winners of the title.

Golf World *said, "'Little Toughie' as The* Atlanta Journal *headline writers call Louise Suggs (how she got that sobriquet is hard to figure. Louise is actually one of the finest examples of a gentle woman) was stroking her way expertly through the 'toughest' field of the year."*

Before I could celebrate my win, I found out that Mom was in the hospital after undergoing surgery for a ruptured disk, news that had been kept from me for several days. My brother Rell said that they chose not to tell me until the last putt dropped for fear of distracting me. I heard the news right after my win and right before I was supposed to do a champion's press conference. I immediately left the course in tears to head home to see Mom, leaving a less than happy press corps. They later understood once the news got out.

The whole week was a strange one for me—first winning the title and then hearing about Mom. What took the biscuit was later learning that, unbeknownst to me, I had also been part of a gambling game called Calcutta, which was outlawed by the USGA. At the time, I was relatively unknown outside of the South and was considered a "field player," so this Calcutta group didn't even contemplate the possibility of me winning until I got to the semis. It made sense later when I remembered this thuggish looking guy in a suit showing up out of the blue and following me for the whole round when I played against Patty Berg. He was able to walk right with me because there were no ropes on the course in those days. And, whenever anyone came close to me, he'd step in and stop them. Apparently, on the last day, the female scorer walking with our group had been warned to stay away from me. Poor thing. She could hardly talk she was so scared. They didn't mess with me directly, but the whole thing still bothered me. At night, there was always someone outside my hotel room in the hallway. It felt like being around the mafia. It was pretty obvious they were protecting their investment.

■　■　■

Later on, in 1949, Louise won the fourth staging of the U.S. Women's Open at Prince George's Country Club in Landover, Maryland, by a record 14 shots from Babe Zaharias. It's a record that still stands in women's golf, and has been bettered by only one player in the men's game; Tiger Woods with his 2000 win at Pebble Beach. Her victory gave the 26-year-old a clean sweep of every major golf tournament possible in the United States and Great Britain.

In the process of winning that first U.S. Women's Open, I got into a zone where it was all just clicking. I was in one of those grooves where everything went right and my whole game was solid. We were playing a course that was longer than they play now. When you take into consideration the equipment we used in those days, it makes it even longer.

We didn't have leaderboards in those days and, because of that, I didn't know where I stood coming down the stretch. However, I knew I was in good shape. If anyone in the gallery said anything about where you stood, you had to try to ignore it because you didn't know if they had the correct information or if they were just messing with you. It wasn't worth the risk. Instead, you just kept in your zone until you were finished. In general, I really didn't need a scoreboard because my approach was always to play the course. No matter what everyone else was shooting, I could only control my own golf shots. If they knocked the ball in the hole, I couldn't do anything about it. Truthfully, I think that's why I was such a good match player; the golf course meant more to me than my opponent.

It's a hard thing to put into words, but when I played well I wasn't thinking about the end result. I was just playing golf. If I won, great. And if I didn't, fine. There wasn't anything more I could do because I always knew I had done my best. I didn't compare tournament victories against each other. However, the exception to that was the 1948 British Ladies' Amateur Championship—my proudest tournament win.

■ ■ ■

In 1953, I traveled over 40,000 miles, not including an exhibition trip I made to Argentina. That season, I won nine titles and almost $20,000. I remember Dad telling me, "Nobody will ever win more money than that." Obviously, that turned out not to be the case but it felt like he was right at the time.

That year, I persuaded Mom and Dad, who were both retired by then and living in an apartment in Atlanta, to travel with me from tournament to tournament. They had never been west of the Mississippi and I told them, "Hey, the tour is going through Texas, Arizona, California and Nevada—why don't you take three months and see that part of the country?" And that's what we did. We packed my car to get everything to fit, and loaded it exactly the same way every time; overnight bags here, my clubs there—you get the picture. We put the hanging clothes in the back seat and rigged it so that they hung over just half the seat, leaving enough room for someone to sit.

I had an air-conditioned car, which made the trip all the more comfortable, and we'd often share the driving. Dad was the only man I've ever known who could get lost in a closet. Whenever he drove and I got in the back seat to sleep, he'd invariably get on the wrong road. Mom would try to tell him, but it was a lost cause.

That trip was a lot of fun and it opened my parents up to new experiences that they wouldn't otherwise have enjoyed. For instance, my friend Dolores Hope knew that we had some time off between tournaments while we were in California, so she invited us to come and stay with her and Bob at their home in Burbank. Bob and Dolores Hope were dear and lifelong friends of mine. For some reason, I've had many nicknames given to me throughout my life. The better known of those is Miss Sluggs; a name given to me by Bob because he thought I hit it so far.

I first met Bob when I was 17 years old. I had just won the Southern Amateur Championship by beating Peg Chandler from Texas in the final. Peg was one of Texas' finest amateur golfers and, at the time, was president of the Women's Southern Golf Association. She was a real class act and definitely a mover and shaker at various levels of society. That year, she had a big exhibition event, benefitting the Red Cross, at Brook Hollow Golf Club in Dallas. It was going to feature celebrities and golfers such as Bob, Bing Crosby, and Babe Zaharias. At the last minute, right before the event, Babe called Peg and asked for appearance money. This was out of the question for a charity event. Well, Babe pulled out and Peg got in touch with me and asked if I'd stand in. I enthusiastically agreed.

What an experience it was for a young kid like me from Austell, Georgia. Over 4,000 tickets had been sold and it was headlined in the local press as the greatest charity event in Dallas' history. That morning, as we were all getting ready to tee off, I was so nervous I could hardly swallow. With adrenaline pumping double-time through every cell of my body, I really let my drive rip right down the first fairway. It even surprised me. Without saying a word, Bob Hope turned around and started marching towards the clubhouse. Bing Crosby called after him and said, "Hey, where do you think you're going?" Without even looking back Bob shouted, "To get a skirt, what do you think?" The whole place just hooted and exploded in laughter. That moment marked the beginning of a tremendous friendship and became the first of many times where I would play Bob's straight man at charity events all across the country. During the war, we went to military bases together to entertain the troops.

Before meeting Bob, I knew I had a sense of humor. I got it from Dad, but didn't really show it off much. As Bob and I did more and more events together, my humor began to show. He always told me that it's not what you say, but how you look and how you say it. There were a couple of moments when he pulled me up on the stage, in front of 5,000 sailors, and asked me a question where I just went blank. Out of the corner of his mouth he'd say, "For God's sake just say something, even if it's nothing." Every once in a while I'd have a flash and come back at him with something smart and I'd get a pretty good laugh, to which he'd say, "Hey, I'm the one who's supposed to get the laughs, not you." He loved it. And so did the audience. For the most part, I learned to keep my mouth shut at the right times because it got to where sometimes I was too quick with the comebacks. He was really supposed to be the funny guy and me his straight man.

As time went on, I really enjoyed (and preferred) being with Bob when he wasn't around people. When there were others around, he was always "on stage." Away from the audience, he could be just as nice as anything. I really became extremely fond of, and close friends with, his wife Dolores. She and I would frequently play golf together at Lakeside Golf Club. She was a pretty good player and would play in the early LPGA events as an amateur—it was a common thing for decent amateurs to fill out our fields.

Dolores really knew how to manage Bob. She used to tease him to no end when he and I would play for dimes and I'd always beat him. Imagine playing Bob Hope for dimes. But that's all I could afford at the time. Because of my young age, Dolores was very protective when I traveled with Bob to the service bases. On one occasion, I was with Dolores in an elevator and the girl operating the elevator looked at me and said, "You're Mr. Hope's girlfriend, ain't ya?" Before I could stammer a shocked reply, Dolores said "Yes, and I'm his wife." That took care of that.

In 1945, Walter Etzel (my boss at Gulf) asked me to arrange a game of golf with Bob Hope. He joked that if I didn't, I'd lose my job. Well, I really didn't want to explore whether that was a joke or not so I said I'd see what I could do. I called Dolores and pleaded, "The boss says that if Bob doesn't play with him, he'll fire me." She just laughed and said, "I doubt that. But let me find out if and when he's going to be in your neck of the woods." As it turned out, he was scheduled to be in Atlanta so I got Dot Kirby to make up the foursome and we played at Capital City Club. I don't know if that's why I kept my job or not, but I was grateful not to have to find out.

When Mom, Dad, and I made the visit to the Hopes' home in California in 1953, the greenskeeper in Dad was immediately excited to find out that the Hopes had a real putting green built in their back yard. Dad had to go out and inspect the type of grass and contours as soon as we arrived. He had not yet met Bob and there was Dad, on his hands and knees looking at the grass, when he saw a pair of feet right beside him. He looked up and said, "Who the hell are you?" To which the owner of the feet replied, "I live here. Who the hell are you?" Of course, it was Bob. That moment stayed a source of humor for both of them going forward. And they got along famously. I know that it was refreshing for Mom and Dad to see that celebrities can be normal people with the same normal family life as anyone else. It was a really enjoyable part of an overall great trip with my folks.

■　■　■

From left: Walter Etzel, Dot Kirby, Bob Hope, and me in 1945 at Capital City Club in Atlanta. Photo courtesy Special Collections and Archives, Georgia State University Library.

Thanks to Alvin Handmacher, who became known as a master patron of women's golf, the Weathervane series of tournaments became the backbone to the LPGA's schedule in the early 1950's. The 144-hole, cross-country competition in 1953 weaved its way from Boca Raton, to Phoenix, on to San Francisco, and ultimately Philadelphia. The combined prize money for the series was $17,000. Louise dominated the tour that year with nine victories, including her fourth Western Open major title—making her by far the season's top money winner with almost $20,000. She alone took $7,445 of the Weathervane prize pot by winning three of the four in the series, along with the $5,000 grand prize for finishing first in the aggregate competition by 11 shots from Patty Berg. Louise capped off the series during torrential rain with an eight-shot win over Patty in the last event at the Whitemarsh

Valley Country Club in Philadelphia. The rain was so heavy that many of the players were calling for a postponement. Not Louise. She, once again, plowed ahead—demonstrating an uncanny ability to play well even in inclement conditions.

Betty McKinnon (left), Betsy Rawls (right), and I take a break from the torrential rain at Whitemarsh Valley Country Club in Philadelphia. Associated Press photo.

■ ■ ■

The 1954 season started with the inaugural $3,500 Sea Island Invitational on the Golden Isles of southern Georgia. The 6,541-yard, par-72 layout proved to be one of the tougher courses of the circuit in those days. And the weather was freezing cold and windy. Unsurprisingly, coming off her banner year in 1953, Louise once again made the most of the weather conditions to top the field as champion. Sea Island had, after all, been her *strategic destination in 1948 to experience playing in windy and cold conditions to prepare for what turned out to be her British Ladies' Amateur and Curtis Cup triumphs. That commitment and determination to prevail against the odds was still paying off.*

A couple of months later in March, bad weather in Georgia turned up again to help Louise bag the 15th Titleholders Championship at Augusta Country Club; her eighth of 11 major championship crowns. Chilly whipping winds, from the tail end of the disastrous Macon tornado, played havoc with the entire field—except Louise. She showed once again that inclement weather couldn't get in her way. She lapped everyone by seven shots and broke Patty Berg's tournament record of 294 by one shot.

Buoyed by these important wins, Louise went on to post five 1954 wins to again lead the tour in victories—tied with her rival Babe Zaharias. In a small stroke of irony, the fifth of those tournament titles came at the Babe Zaharias Open in Beaumont, where she beat the tournament namesake by two shots.

In 1954, the LPGA's fifth official year since incorporating, the number of professionals was growing. January's Sea Island event was an historic moment for women's professional golf with a record of 19 professionals competing. The flip side of that progress also meant that it was the first time an open golf tournament had to leave some of the women out of the money, since LPGA regulations at the time stated that only the top 11 professionals could receive a paycheck. It was becoming clear that players without endorsement contracts were not getting by financially. Betty Hicks barely won just over $1,000 in prize money but, after deducting her expenses, she was just $10 ahead. Unless a player was in the top four on the money list, it was difficult to balance winnings without extra income. As it was, the top players were able to live off their salaries from sponsors, royalties, and per diem expenses, but such deals were few and far between. It was a tough road for the journeywomen of the tour. I really give credit to the players who didn't have sponsors.

They hung on and we all rallied to support each other. That kind of compassionate culture in the beginning is what helped make the tour what it is today.

■ ■ ■

The 1956 Titleholders was, once again, dampened by bad weather for everyone except for Louise. It was freezing cold in the first round. A field of players that hadn't expected the bitter conditions was taken by surprise and wasn't properly attired. Cindy Howard, from Connecticut, teed off in shorts and was so cold on the first hole that she made a nine. A writer from the Atlanta Constitution *kindly went to his car and found a pair of pants that he delivered to her on the course. Horrific weather again came into play during the second round, when 45 mile-an-hour winds and early morning rains made Augusta Country Club tough going. Undaunted, Louise lived up to her reputation as an inclement-condition champion and triumphed to get her third of four Titleholders titles. The highlight of the week was when her golfing idol, Bobby Jones, presented her the trophy.*

■ ■ ■

A packed schedule of 27 events worth $202,200, almost 30 percent more than the previous year, made 1959 a banner year for the young LPGA. It was the first of an impressive three-season run for Louise. The year also was a standout for Betsy Rawls, who won a record amount of prize money (with $26,235) and 10 tournament victories—two better than the tour's previous season record of eight. Despite this, many felt that Louise's year was superior. Although she only won three times she was victorious in the Titleholders tournament, which, in those days, was considered "the big one." Louise and Betsy had gone head-to-head on the final stretch of the event. Louise shot what was considered a brilliant closing round of 71 for what she termed, "One of the greatest I have ever played when I knew I had to play one."

In addition to her three wins, Louise posted nine runner-up finishes. She started out the year with a 13th-place finish in Tampa and was seventh the following week. After that, she only finished out of the top four once, when she came in sixth in the Western Open. In short, in 21 tournament starts, she was out of the top four on only three occasions, and never out of the top 13. It resulted in Louise leading the season's Performance Average, a statistical ranking sponsored by Golf Digest that was used to determine the top players of the time—not unlike today's Rolex World Golf Rankings. The final unofficial analysis for 1959 was that Louise topped the season with statistics, and Betsy was first with money and tournament wins.

Louise also came close to winning the 1959 Vare Trophy for Scoring Average. She had the season's lowest average of 73.58, to Betsy's 74.03, but fell a fraction short of winning the Trophy because of the award's requirement of playing in at least 80 percent of eligible tournaments. Sadly, it was the act of doing a good deed for a tournament that ultimately cost her the honor.

I agreed to do a pre-tournament radio interview in Cleveland for the $10,000 Alliance Machine International Open in Alliance, just south of the city. At the end of the interview, the tournament chairman thanked me for my time and then declared to me, "I'll see you at the cocktail party tonight." Well, I hadn't brought any dressy clothes with me and I told him I couldn't possibly come to the event in the casual attire I was wearing. When he told me if I didn't come to the party I couldn't play in the tournament, I decided just that—to not play in the tournament. I really felt that it was important to make a point. It wasn't that I didn't want to help the tournament, otherwise why would I have taken the time to do the radio interview? And that extra tournament would have given me the number of tournaments I needed to win the Vare Trophy.

■ ■ ■

The following year (in 1960), Louise came up against Mickey Wright, one of the LPGA players she most admired in competition. With four wins and 15 top-four finishes, Louise led the money list with $16,892, just $512 ahead of Mickey. But Louise was barely beaten in the Vare Trophy again, this time because of Mickey's incredible year of 10 wins, including three major championships.

■ ■ ■

Louise's three-season run of remarkable performances reached its pinnacle in 1961. She came into the year considered the weekly favorite to win. It was like she was making the LPGA Tour her own private bank. She began by, once again, winning on Sea Island. Then she took victory in Naples, Florida. Out of her first seven tournaments, she captured five titles and was second in the other two—to none other than Mickey Wright. The Suggs-Wright show had created a storyline about the steel grip they seemed to have on the tour. Louise became the first player to win a tournament three consecutive years when she clinched the Dallas Civitan Open by five shots over Mickey after birdieing four of the last seven holes over the rain-swept Glen Lakes Country Club. With over $19,000 in winnings from seven titles, she came in second with earnings behind Mickey, who was the 1961 leading money winner for the first of four consecutive years.

"My idea of rhythmic beauty in a golf swing would be spelled 'Louise Suggs,'" said Mickey Wright. "Louise was my favorite person to play with. Whenever I learned that we were paired together, I'd say, 'Oh good, I get to play with you today. I get to watch that swing and maybe pick up some of your rhythm.' And then Louise would tease me and say, 'You'd better not look—you'd better not look.'"

The respect between the two legends is mutual.

In my opinion, Mickey Wright has the best woman's swing ever. I have always admired it. She's tall, had a beautiful arc, and was a master of hitting the golf ball. People don't talk enough about

Mickey's ball striking. It's what helped her win so many tournaments. She could make carries that the rest of us couldn't even consider. Instead we would have to go around the corner.

My favorite people to play with were Mickey, Betsy Rawls, and Marlene Hagge. I liked to play quickly, and Marlene was fast and kept it moving. Mickey and Betsy were both great players, were quiet, and just played their own games. That's how I liked to be in competition.

Whenever Mickey and I played with one another we seemed to play our best golf. I was runner-up in the U.S. Women's Open on four occasions, and two of them were to Mickey. While I would rather have won, I respected losing to someone like her. Two of the greatest rounds of golf I ever saw a woman play were by Mickey when she won the 1961 U.S. Women's Open at Baltusrol. In those days, we used to play 36 holes on the final day of the Championship. On this occasion, I happened to be paired with Mickey and we were playing pretty much from the tips of Baltusrol's Lower Course—a layout on which you had to earn everything you got. Those 36 holes were almost like an endurance test. I kept up with her pretty well over the first 18, but she just beat me down on the second round. She played some of the finest golf shots I've ever seen hit by a woman and she made a lot of ungodly putts. It was one of those moments where all I could do was stand there and watch. It was like I was part of the gallery. She played magnificently.

■　■　■

"Oh, Good Grief, Men! You Let A Woman Beat You?"—UPI *Headline*

Louise's third tournament victory of 1961 was a showstopper. While she didn't win a major that year, she might as well have as evidenced by the headlines that rippled throughout the sports world when she topped the entire field at the Royal Poinciana Invitational Championship. The

$10,000 event featured a roster of both men and women: PGA players like Sam Sneed, Dow Finsterwald, and Gardner Dickinson; and LPGA players Mickey Wright, Marlene Hagge, Betsy Rawls, and Patty Berg, among others. It was the first time a woman had defeated male professionals in any sport—and from the same tees no less. She shot 156, six under par—one better than Dub Pagan and two better than Sam Snead. And that was with a bogey on the last hole.

The event was played at the plush Palm Beach Par-3 Golf Club, which was owned and developed by Mike Phipps, who put on the 54-hole event to help publicize his newly opened property. It was one of a number of events played during that era featuring men and women together. In progressive style, the top woman earned the same $1,200 as the top man, but the prize money for the women only went six players deep, to the men's 12 ($6,000 for the men and $4,000 for the women). Quite a crowd of Palm Beach's celebrities and socialites turned out to watch us play.

Needless to say, me winning turned out to be a shocker for everyone, not least of all Sam Snead. In the scorer's tent afterward, Sam asked, "What were you trying to do out there? This was just an exhibition!" He just kept on complaining, even in the clubhouse, to the point where I finally had enough and said, "Sam, I was trying to win a golf tournament. Clearly you weren't. I don't know what the hell you're bitching about. You weren't even second." Well, that made all the other guys, who seemed okay with me winning, hoot with laughter. Not Sam. He was a macho guy and he didn't like it one bit. He didn't even take his spikes off before jumping in his car and squealing out of that parking lot, leaving all kinds of burned rubber on the road.

Because the course was a par-3, the win proved to me that a putter could be a woman golfer's deadliest weapon. Don't get me wrong. The course wasn't some little pitch and putt. In fact, you had to really think about your shots because the ocean frontage brought some tricky wind into play. One day, on the 10th hole, I had to take a 4-wood and almost holed it. With that said, the shorter length of the holes took the strength advantage away from the men, so it came down to a real test of skill on the short game. I used to assert that women didn't work on their short game as much as men—a mistake, because nothing is more challenging than putting and more important to your final score. It's pretty much a fact that it's the player who putts well throughout a tournament that usually wins. Obviously, I putted well that week.

Runner-up Dub Pagan with me after I beat a field of men and women in the 1961 Royal Poinciana Invitational. Photo courtesy Golf Digest Resource Center.

■ ■ ■

"Louise Suggs will not turn into a pillar of salt when she leaves the circuit. She'll make the decision easily and with her own sense of logic when the time comes. And she will never look back."—Golf Digest, *August 1961*

In 1962, at the age of 38, I made the decision to quit full-time competitive play. As great as 1961 was for me, it just wasn't as much fun any more. Golf had begun to feel like a job. After all the years of grinding to help get the Tour going, and keep it running, I was extremely fatigued. I had become tired of playing and wasn't practicing as much any more. It had gotten to the point were a typical day might include an appearance at a clothing store, sandwiched between exhibitions at clubs 35 miles apart. Add to that the pressures of regular tournament play with heady expectations put on a top player and it became completely exhausting. During an interview about my great year in 1961, I remember saying that I just hoped I'd have enough sense to quit when golf became an out-and-out chore to play. I knew deep down at the time of the interview that I wasn't knocking myself out like I used to. I was just flat tired.

All of the years of travel, work, pressure, and competition just caught up with me. With the exception of my friend Jean, nobody could tell because I just kept showing up and winning tournaments. However, it got to the point when I finally had to give in. I was completely and utterly physically and emotionally exhausted. I was so spent and depleted that I decided to take some time and see a doctor for the sake of my health. Because that meant missing a tournament I'd committed to playing, I had my doctor write a letter explaining my situation. Apparently the letter never got into the hands of the LPGA's powers-that-be and they fined me $25. It was an impossible pill for me to swallow. The letter was never returned to the doctor so I have always believed it was, in fact, delivered correctly. The amount of the fine wasn't the point. It was only $25. It was the principle of the thing. After all the years of work, dedication, and more than enough demonstration of integrity, it felt like the greatest affront. They didn't give me the benefit of the doubt that I'd done the right thing, and it all came at a time when I was just so tired of the grind. The fine made me realize I'd had enough and just didn't want to do it any more. And so I quit.

After I made my decision, I began missing the competition. However, I didn't want to return to the game full-time so, for a number of years, I periodically played on tour in some of my favorite events or where some of my favorite people lived. It was nice to be in a position to be able to do that.

■ ■ ■

Louise's first step back to periodic tournament play after her retirement was the following July—at the 1963 U.S. Women's Open Championship at Kenwood Country Club in Cincinnati. Despite the fact it had been over a year since she'd been in the heat of competition, Louise demonstrated again what a great U.S. Open player she was by tying for second, three shots behind champion Mary Mills.

■ ■ ■

In addition to winning the 1949 and 1952 titles, to this day Louise still holds a number of Open records: the largest victory margin of victory with 14 shots; the most top-five finishes with 14 (Mickey Wright is second with 10); and, the most top-10's with 19 (Kathy Whitworth is second with 14). Her record of top-10s includes a consecutive string of 11 (another current record) starting in 1953 that featured four runner-up positions and four others in the top five.

In 1967, Louise again rose to the occasion at the U.S. Women's Open. At the age of 44, and despite playing in only a handful of tournaments each year, she teed it up over the Cascades Course at The Homestead in Hot Springs, Virginia. She finished tied for fourth, three back from a young French amateur, Catherine Lacoste. Lacoste had a five-stroke lead after 36 and 54 holes. Louise was nine shots back going into the final round, but was

poised to mount a charge. After 15 holes, Louise had methodically narrowed
the gap to just one shot.

That Championship was one of the first times women's golf was televised. Byron Nelson and Chris Schenkel were commentating from a booth set up so that they could see action on the 15th, 16th, 17th, and 18th holes. On the par-3 15th, I was in a nice position for a birdie and I was getting ready to stand over my putt. Because all the doors and windows to the announcers' booth were open, I could hear Byron's voice. It wasn't bothering me until I heard him say, "I've never seen anybody make this difficult putt. It's very tricky." Well, I stopped, backed off, and said, "Byron, which way does it break?" Dead silence. He shut up and I made the putt.

I was now only one shot back and had great momentum coming into the 16th hole, which is a funny hole. It's a par-5, dogleg to the right, with a spring running by the putting surface. I drove it down the right center, and followed it with a second shot into perfect position. Unfortunately, I buried my third shot in the bank near the spring and, in trying to get it out, I exploded it over the green. I finally got it on the green and took a seven. In that moment, my mistake let Catherine pull away from me. By winning that Championship, she became the only amateur ever to win a U.S. Women's Open.

■   ■   ■

The remainder of my professional playing days really came down to showing up to a handful of events here and there. These were tournaments that either were close to home or had some significant meaning to me, such as the Dinah Shore in Palm Springs—which is now called the Kraft Nabisco Championship. I had played in the first Dinah in 1983, and because many of the folks in the area were dear friends of mine, such as Bob and Dolores Hope, the event always was a particularly fun week for me. I enjoyed playing there right up until the late 1980's.

My Tools for the Game

It would be fascinating to see how today's professionals would fare with the kind of equipment we played and with the course conditions we experienced. It would certainly give perspective as to how much the game has changed and evolved over the decades.

I feel strongly that the modern golf ball is too hot. Never in my born days would I have expected to see anyone hit the ball well over 300 yards—and it's not just one person, it's commonplace. Even the women are hitting it around 280 yards. If I hit a ball 250, that was a tremendous drive. And I was considered one of the longer hitters. Because of this new distance off the tee, they've had to make changes to (and then ruin) some of the great old courses like Merion, Baltusrol, and Augusta.

In addition to the ball, the way they make equipment by pouring clubs in a mold has made everything so uniform. Modern clubs make it hard to manufacture shots, unless you're really strong like Tiger Woods. I'm sad to say that, outside of Tiger, there really aren't any shot makers any more.

The modern professional also has the tremendous benefit of having a permanent caddie—which is something we just didn't have. We had to take local caddies from week to week and you never knew whom you were going to get. I have no doubt it would have made a big difference to us old-timers; you get to know the caddie, they get to know you, and it relieves a lot of the pressure. I don't think people realize how much of an impact a good caddie can make—a difference of at least three to five strokes per round. I look back at the situation with my caddie Tish when I won the British Ladies Amateur. Trusting in his advice proved to be the difference between winning and not.

Today's top players don't have to worry about such variables. Most of them have regular caddies and equipment company reps, along with tour trucks that make sure their clubs and balls are dialed exactly the way they want them. At the end of the day, it really comes down to the player and their ability to execute shots. But the value of good and consistent equipment cannot be understated.

I won't say that I've always known a lot about equipment, but I knew what I liked and I knew how to work with a club designer. Photo by Horace Heley.

The irons I hit in my heyday were like toothpicks compared to modern equipment. In the beginning, they were mostly wooden-shafted. The iron heads were like slivers with a really thin topline, which I've always liked. I always felt that with a small-headed iron or wood in my hands, I was more inclined to swing at the ball and that really worked for me. You had to be strong to hit them a long way.

Throughout my career I played with a C9 swing weight, which was considered a lightweight men's club with a lightweight shaft. The action in my clubs was up under the grip—not down by the tip. I couldn't play with a flexible tip because my hands were so active I couldn't control it.

I won't say that I've always known a lot about equipment, but I knew what I liked and I knew how to work with a club designer. When I represented MacGregor, I worked with their head designer, Tony Penna. He was really ahead of his time in those days— introducing design ideas like putting color on faces. The only thing that I ever took a really strong stand on with Tony was the fact that they made the women's clubs too short. You can always choke a club but you can't lengthen it. When they made women's clubs in those days, they'd basically just take a set of lightweight men's clubs, cut them down, and that was the woman's club. There was no such thing as fitting for women.

In my early days as an amateur, I played with a mish-mash of just about whatever anyone gave me. My first set was one that Dad sawed down for me, with bicycle tape on the grips. Those clubs included a Wright and Ditson 7-iron that someone just walked up and handed to me one day at Lithia. Wright and Ditson was a premier brand of sports equipment and clothing from the early 1900's. That 7-iron was the most lofted club I had for a while and I absolutely loved it. I could eat soup off that thing. It was small-headed and I could do just about anything with it. It's the club I used when I learned to get out of bunkers. And because of that, I could use a 7-iron from anywhere—to a lot of folks' amazement.

When I first started playing the amateur championships, another of my special individual clubs was a wooden-shafted one-iron. I just loved it and could hit it from anywhere. It was a Spalding Kro-Flight that had been one of Dad's clubs, and it was the best feeling club I ever had. And, it was also the worst looking.

Sadly, I hung it on a root one day and it shattered. I just about cried to lose it.

My first full set of matched clubs was by Kroydon—which later became part of Ram Golf. They were all the rage at the time. These were my first steel-shafted clubs and were purchased out of a catalog by Bob Morgan, a close family friend at Lithia. When I was younger, Bob used to help me with my golf swing. He figured that those clubs would fit me better than any of the others. And he was right.

As I outgrew the Kroydons, I moved on to a set of Bobby Jones clubs made by Spalding. I got them from a guy named Gus Novotny, who was a sales rep for Spalding and then later for MacGregor. Gus would call on the golf shop at Lithia and would adjust his schedule so that we'd be the last stop on his rounds—right before dinner. We always knew why. He loved Mom's cooking and was always hoping for Miss Marguerite's special fried chicken. Gus had the grips on those clubs put on inside out so they'd be rough and tacky since I didn't wear a glove. When I first started playing they didn't make gloves, so I just never got the feel for wearing one. I tried leftover gloves that people left around the pro shop from time to time, but I couldn't feel the club. My hands were my game. Golf, to me, has always been about feel. If I couldn't feel the club, I couldn't do anything with it. So, I never used a glove my whole career.

My favorite clubs over the course of my entire career is a set of wooden ones that is now on display in the Louise Suggs Library at Cherokee Town and Country Club in Atlanta. The set includes a steel-shafted driver, and a 2, 3, and 4-wood, all made completely out of dogwood by a great club maker called Bert Dargie. I met Bert in 1941 when I was 17 and playing in the Southern Amateur in Memphis. I had seen this guy following me and he eventually came up and introduced himself. It turned out that Bert was a Scotsman who had moved from St Andrews and had set up his own clubmaking business in Memphis. He worked with some of the game's greats like Ben Hogan and Arnold Palmer.

After Bert introduced himself, he told me that he'd like to make me a set of woods. I told him I'd have to politely decline since I couldn't afford them on the $25 a week I was earning working for Gulf—and I certainly didn't want to jeopardize my amateur standing with the USGA by taking them for free. Well, he went ahead and made them anyway. When he sent them to me, he included an invoice for $25 and left it up to me what I wanted to do. I paid the $25 and went on to use those beautiful Bert Dargie clubs with "L.S." engraved on the sole for the rest of my amateur career. Those clubs were so special to me you couldn't have paid me a million dollars to give them up. When I turned professional and signed with MacGregor, they had a heck of a time making me a set of woods to suit me like those Dargies.

Dogwood is about is the hardest wood there is. As such, there is no need for an insert. When you got a clean hit with them, the ball really takes off. Even after all those years, all those tournaments, all of those rounds, those Dargies look hardly used. People often ask about the clubs and say, "If they are so great, how come more people didn't play with dogwood?" Well, to make a wood head, you have to carve it out of a single block of wood, and most dogwood trees aren't big enough to provide a sufficiently large block without a knot.

My woods weren't the only treasured clubs to see me through my amateur victories—my putter was a cherished weapon too. Our family friend, Dr. Frank Clark, gave me a Walter Hagen steel spiral shaft putter that I used my whole amateur career. Back in my day, greens weren't as smooth and slick as they are now. Because of that, most putters were blade heads with a slight loft so that you could get the ball up and rolling. Dr. Clark didn't like that putter and just gave it away—my gain, for sure. I gave it to the USGA a number of years ago to display in their museum.

For the most part, the golf balls I played with left a lot to be desired. At one point in the 1930's, there was a golf ball called the Ugly Duckling, made by Spalding. I remember someone gave me a bunch of new ones. The Ugly Duckling was one of the first balls to feature dimples of different sizes. Whoever gave them to me obviously bought a bunch of them and evidently didn't like them. So I inherited them. I quickly found out why. They were terrible. I can still picture that Ugly Duckling in the sky on certain shots. That ball should never have been on the market. They got the name right for sure—ugly.

After I turned professional and signed with MacGregor, the company decided to make their own golf balls under the Tourney name. We were told that we didn't have to play with it while it was still in development, but they went on to stress that they needed our input and would appreciate it if we could play the ball as much as we could. Well, Byron Nelson and I played with it. We discussed it once and he told me, "It's cost me tournaments and I know it's cost you as well." I agreed. I would hit one every once in a while and, I kid you not, it would go out of round in the air—goose egg-shaped—right before your eyes. It was tough until they finally produced a good ball. And through it all, Byron and I remained loyal to the brand.

One year before The Masters, we all got a letter from MacGregor saying the company executives had decided that the Tourney ball was now playable and, as staff members, we had to play it. At the time, almost everyone except Byron and I was playing the Spalding Dot. I was glad that I didn't have to worry about going through the switch because I'd been playing with the clunker the whole time. The Masters came along and MacGregor's president, Henry Cowen, invited me to come along to help drive around and entertain the company's customers. I was with him when we came across Ben Hogan with three Titleist balls in his hands. I heard Mr. Cowen say, "Ben, we've decided." To which Ben said, "No. I don't think so." Mr.

Cowen insisted, "Ben, if you tee that up, you're fired." Well, sure enough, he did tee it up. I don't know exactly how the story shook out afterward, but Ben Hogan left MacGregor that year and ended up with his own equipment company.

I know that I would have played better and perhaps won more with a better ball in play. I just knew if a ball was good or not—that's how good my sense of feel was. For example, we had a rain delay one time somewhere in Iowa and I was hanging around in the locker room with Marlene Hagge, putting some balls on the carpet to pass the time. I said to her, "This ball is smaller than the other two." Marlene scoffed, saying it was ridiculous to think I could tell the difference. So I said, "I'll bet you a dollar," to which she replied, "I'll bet you five dollars." We went in the pro shop and got a ball ring to measure it. Well it was, in fact, smaller than the other balls. Marlene laughed and said, "Well good grief. No wonder you can putt."

The Swing—Hands, Feel, and Imagination

"Louise's swing combines all the desirable elements of efficiency, timing, and coordination. It appears to be completely effortless. Yet, despite her slight build, she is consistently as long off the tee and through the fairway as any of her feminine contemporaries in competitive golf. And no one is right down the middle any more than this sweet-swinging Georgia miss." Ben Hogan

I didn't have any formal swing instruction. Most of what I learned came from watching and emulating the golf swings of players I admired—like Bobby Jones. I inherited a great sense of feel from Dad and he really encouraged me to tap into it. He told me that golf was like baseball—nobody could tell a pitcher how to produce a fast curve or a slow one; they simply had to learn by doing it. We spent numerous hours together working by trial and error with tips he'd picked up in books, magazines, or just by talking to folks. In the end, it came down to what felt right to me.

Later on, I got some help from a family friend, Bob Morgan—a good golfer from Austell who lived about half a mile up the road from the golf course. He used to walk by the range every now and again and give me tips. Eventually, he went to Dad and said, "Do you mind if I work with her?" Dad replied, "Sure, I've taught her everything I know." Bob gave me a great deal of insight into the game. He was a big advocate of me using my hands and he showed me how to hit hooks and slices, and how to get out of tight lies.

My game became mostly about hands. The more I played and the more I practiced, the more I felt the club. That's not necessarily the case for today's players. Because of the way they now make

Most of what I learned came from watching and emulating the golf swings of players I admired.

balls and clubs, it's almost impossible to move the ball around with your hands—unless you are extremely strong. While some male players are able to do it, only a few top women players can. I think it's a shame because, in my opinion, the game is supposed to be played differently than it is today. Unfortunately, it's almost become a science.

Bobby Jones said to me, "If you've got a good grip, unless you line up incorrectly, it's almost impossible to hit the ball badly." Because of that, I've always believed that the hands are the most important part of the golf swing. If the grip is correct, you've got a good chance to begin with. If it's wrong, you've got no chance at all. I always made sure that my grip was as good as it could be and then

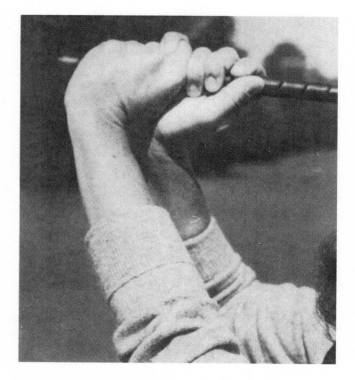

I've always believed that the golf swing begins with a solid grip.

decided what I was going to do to get the clubhead started. Once I made up my mind—that was it. I didn't think about anything else.

I learned through experience that I could hit the ball any way I wanted if I felt the shot. Getting that feel is important because it's not possible to concentrate on every mechanical part of a golf swing. You don't have time to think from takeaway to impact. Stewart Maiden, Bobby Jones' teacher who once came to observe me practicing, told me, "When I am hitting a golf ball, I can think of exactly one thing— hitting the golf ball."

Golfers make it far too complicated. I used to have a lot of people ask, "What do you think about when you hit the golf ball?" And I'd say, "Not a dang thing." When I was playing, I figured I would either hit the ball or miss it. Really. Once I set myself up for the shot, I couldn't worry about it any more—either before or after the stroke. I knew that whatever the outcome of the shot, there was always another one coming up.

Before I even set foot on a golf course, I knew I could rely on a mental picture of my golf swing. Because of this, I was able to produce the same swing almost all of the time, which really helped when I was under pressure. I would think of my swing like a wagon wheel; with my head as the axis and my arms and legs as the spokes. With this image in mind, I got a smooth, fluid swing with everything working together. It's much easier to have a mental picture of your swing than having to memorize a whole host of instructions.

Having a good imagination went hand-in-hand with sense of feel as essential parts of my game. Once I was out on the course, I could visualize how I wanted each shot to go—then I just had to believe it and trust my intuition. For example, when Dot Kirby and I played each other in the final of the 1947 Western Open at Capital City Club, it was pouring rain. By the time we got to the fifth green, the cup was covered with running water. I saw that if I putted into the direction of the running water, it would roll with the water in the direction of the cup. With that image in mind, I made the stroke and, sure enough, it went in. I quickly had to take it out of the water-filled cup before it could float out again. I knew that if I had putted it at the hole, the strength of the water stream would have carried it off line. It simply came down to visualization and then a commitment to the shot.

I recall a similar moment on my way to winning the 1954 Titleholders Championship at Augusta Country Club. We always played the event in the spring—when the weather wasn't warm enough for the Bermuda grass to fill in. As a result, we had to deal with a lot of cuppy lies. In the final round, I got to my drive on the 10th hole and discovered that I had one of those lies. I was 170 yards from the pin, and because of how my ball was sitting, it looked like

I had an impossible shot. I said to my caddie, "I can't get it up in the air from that lie, so I think that the best thing for me to do is take a 2-iron and try to run it up there through the opening in front of the green." And that's exactly how I played the shot. I just knocked the fool out of it. The ball never got more than three or four feet off the ground before running up to about five feet from the hole. After putting out, I walked off the green towards Dad, who was waiting for me. He said, "Sis, that was a hell of a miss," to which I replied, "Dad, I played it that way on purpose." By the time I got to the next tee, I looked back at the 10th hole and saw Dad standing on the spot from where I'd hit the shot. He was trying to see what kind of divot I'd made. I don't think he ever believed that I actually intended to hit it that way.

During a 1953 tournament in San Diego, Mom and Dad (who had been traveling with me that season) were following each of my rounds. We got to a hole where I missed the green to the left and ended up on a hard-packed dirt service road. The green was elevated—almost to where it was on a shelf. By the time I got to my ball, Dad had already walked past it and assessed the situation. I had to hit it pretty much straight up—about 45 feet. Well, as it turned out I could see the shot I needed to hit. I had to flip it and try to hit the ball and the road at the same time. It worked. I later found out that Dad had decided that I didn't have any chance at a shot. "I don't know how in the heck you got the ball up and onto that green. How on earth did you know to do that?" he asked me. The best way I could describe it to him was, "Imagine if you wanted to throw a baseball up there from the same spot. You wouldn't just haul back and throw it—you'd flip it with your hands. My golf shot was the same way." When I put it that way, he understood. It was all about feel and imagination.

I was fortunate to have been blessed with an innate sense of rhythm, which really helped my golf game. When I was about 30,

I was at a dance with a group of friends and a man I didn't know asked me to dance. I agreed, and when we came back to the table, he said, "Ladies and gentlemen, I just danced with a ghost." I looked at him and said, "What do you mean by that?" He explained, "You were so light on your feet. It was like there was nothing in my arms. And the way you followed me was like you were completely connected to the music and just knew where I was going to go." I thought about it and realized that was also the way I played golf.

Throughout my playing and teaching career, I developed a number of approaches to the game that helped me—one of them being a different way to practice for a tournament. I found that whenever many of the LPGA players got to a new golf course at the beginning of the week, they'd either run to the driving range and beat balls or go out and play the golf course. For me, that didn't always seem the most productive use of time. Instead, I began my tournament preparation by walking the golf course in reverse—without clubs. I started at the 18th green and then walked backwards down each hole. You get an entirely different perspective. You see trouble areas that aren't always obvious from the tee or the fairway. You'll be amazed at what you can accomplish without even hitting a shot if you do this in lieu of a practice round. On other days, if it rained and we couldn't practice, I would sit in my motel room and think, shot by shot, how I would play the entire course. The time to practice is not when you go to the golf course. If you haven't learned what you need to know by the time you get there, it's too late.

Another "go to" staple for my game, when I felt that my swing was out of whack, was to put my feet together, get my grip right, and then stand and hit the ball while trying to keep my balance. Once I began to feel that I was hitting it solidly, I would begin to spread my feet a little bit more each time. It helped me to keep my head still, swing within myself, and not lunge at the ball. Even when I was in the middle of a competitive round, if I began missing the ball or couldn't focus, I would put my feet together and hit the ball that way on the golf course. People would look at me and say, "What's the matter with you? Are you crazy?" But their comments didn't bother me. I was just trying to get my swing and game back together and, more often than not, it worked.

I once had a student who just couldn't hit a chip shot. It got so bad that one day I just told her to close her eyes and hit it. It worked. From that moment on, that woman hit every chip shot with her eyes closed. She said that she was able to really feel the shot. So, when you're trying to get in touch with the true feel of a stroke, just close your eyes.

I'll share one more simple thought on an age-old instruction tip—one that so many golfers execute incorrectly. How many times do you hear, "Just keep your eye on the ball?" Well, what they don't tell you is—which part of the ball? As a result, most golfers just stare at the top of the ball. Unfortunately, if that's what you focus on, that's exactly what you'll hit. The top of the ball! I always used to look at the back of the ball because that's what I wanted to hit. I learned this because when Bobby Jones began playing golf at the age of six, he would tee up the ball with the logo in the rear so that he would have something specific on which to focus at address. So simple and yet so effective.

"Don't kill the ball—just swing easy. That's what every pro told me. But just as quickly as they gave me their advice, I'd go right ahead and try to murder the ball. It took a tiny smiling she-Rebel from down Georgia way to reassure me beyond all doubt that you can hit those sizzling drives with a minimum of effort." Jack Fleischer, Bridgeport Sunday Herald, *July 1949*

There's Only One Way to Do It—the Right Way

"Louise is truly one of a kind in the sense that I've never known Louise to say anything that wasn't exactly what she believed—in unmistakable language. She is as intellectually honest a human being as I have ever known." Charles S. Mechem, Jr. LPGA Commissioner Emeritus

There are many layers in getting to know the entirety of Louise Suggs. First comes the truth. Once truth has been established, then comes trust. If that trust is unbroken, then the fiercest of loyalties emerges and that loyalty leads to great love. Once you have earned Louise's trust, loyalty, and love, she will give all of it to you in abundance. And always will as long as it is always fueled by one thing—the truth.

Whether she was winning or losing on the golf course, helping build a professional golf tour, making friends, or just going shopping, one overarching influence—a true North Star—has always guided Louise Suggs in every single thing she does. She believes in the truth, the whole truth, and nothing but the truth. To Louise, honesty has been the epicenter for each act and every interaction throughout her life. It is unwavering and unconditional. Her first assumption has always been, and always will be, that everyone else is the same. Trust in others has led to disappointment many times. And when it has, Louise, in no uncertain terms, let her disapproval be known. She shoots her arrow of truth in a straight line and leaves no doubt as to what she believes is the right thing. No politicking, no couching, no softening the edges—just the facts ma'am. You can like it or lump it, but you are never going to be confused as to where you stand with Louise Suggs.

All of the things I believe in, and how I act on all of them, I attribute to Mom and Dad. Even today, when I do something I'll stop and think, "Hmm. Mom wouldn't have liked that," or, "What would Dad think?" I learned from Dad that how you comport yourself in sports is an indication of how you generally act in life. He often said to me, "Sis, I'll tell you one thing, if you open your mouth, be sure that whatever comes out of it is honest. If you do that, you may get in trouble, but you won't be in trouble for long." And that's the way I've tried to be. I've never intentionally maligned anyone, but I have to speak my mind if I think it's right. All of my life I've known that I can't stand hypocrisy. I believe that integrity will win every time—maybe not at first, but eventually it wins out. And that has helped me. I've always been able to sleep well at night knowing that I've said what I needed to say. If I realize that I haven't said or done the right thing, I guarantee I go back and fix it.

"You always know where you stand with Louise Suggs," said Ty Votaw, former LPGA Commissioner, and Executive Vice President—Chief Global Communications Officer for the PGA Tour. "She's a straight shooter and she calls it as she sees it. With that honesty comes integrity. I've been told by her peers that Louise carried everything she did with a quiet dignity and grace, almost to her detriment in that she didn't get nearly enough credit for the things that she did and accomplished. She had, in her playing days, a genuine empathy for her fellow playing competitors, feeling their bad luck or misfortune—especially if she gained from that misfortune."

There is no greater example of Louise's concern for her fellow competitors than an incident at the 1963 U.S. Women's Open at Kenwood Country Club in Cincinnati—a moment where another player's misfortune could have turned to Louise's gain. Instead, it became a demonstration of the sportsmanship that Louise believes defines the game of golf.

I had retired from full-time competitive play in 1962 but still showed up for some of the bigger tournaments. Mary Mills, a heck of a good player who had only turned pro the year before and had won the Rookie of the Year Award, went into the final round three shots ahead of me. We were paired together on that last day and Joe Dey was officiating our group. Coming down the stretch, we got to the par-3 16th and we were both on the green. I was away first but Mary's ball mark was on my line, so I asked if she'd move it a few inches to one side—which she did. When it was her turn to putt, I noticed that she had forgotten to replace her mark back to the original spot and was about to take the stroke. Even Joe hadn't noticed. I quickly spoke up and told Mary just in time and she got the chance to re-mark the ball. If she'd mistakenly gone ahead and putted from the wrong place she would have been assessed a two-stroke penalty—which could have changed momentum and how the leaderboard shook out. It wasn't my responsibility to say anything, but how on earth would I have slept at night? It makes me sick to this day to even think about it. I only ever wanted to win fair and square and intentionally letting her trip on an innocent ruling mistake wasn't the way to do it. To me, it would have felt like I'd cheated. She played the best, she shot the lowest score, and she deserved to win.

Now on the other side of the coin, if I ever saw someone knowingly bend, manipulate, or flat-out break a rule, you were going to hear about it! A perfect example of this took place in 1956 when I saw an established player take advantage of the late Ruth Jessen who, at the time, was a young, inexperienced rookie. Ruth turned professional at the age of 20 and moved from her hometown of Seattle to Cincinnati to work for MacGregor and play the tour on their behalf. In those days, if you were 20 you weren't old enough to work without a guardian. So, the head of MacGregor, Henry Cowen, told me, "Okay Louise, you are now her guardian." I said, "What?" But, that was that. He'd already made up his mind. After she joined the tour, Ruth and I were paired together in Sarasota with one of the top players of that era. When we got to the 18th hole, I was on the right side of the fairway and the two of them were on the left side in the rough. I saw and heard the other player say to Ruth, "In Florida, you have this Spanish moss," and she reached up to the Spanish moss that was hanging from the tree and in the way of her shot. As she did it, she said, "Ruth, this is dead isn't it?" And pulled it down.

Well it wasn't dead, and she improved her position by moving it. At that point, I wasn't going to get in the middle of that mess and I wasn't the one keeping the other player's card. However, when we finished, I said to that player, "Hey, you've been living and playing golf in Florida most of your life and you know good and well that moss wasn't dead. Why don't you do the right thing?" Well, despite me saying my piece, she still didn't do the right thing. She just took advantage of young Ruth who, at the time, didn't know better. However, I collared Ruth later and let her have it about how she needed to learn the rules and stand up to other players. I handed her a Rules of Golf book and said, "Now, learn it." Later on, when she got a bit braver, she told me, "Louise, I wasn't literally whipped but it surely felt like it when you got through with me." I know that experience made a difference to her going forward.

During a tournament in Virginia Beach, I hit into a par-3 and the ball plugged right off the green. We were playing preferred lies so we were allowed to clean and replace the ball. I cleaned the ball and put it back into the plugged hole. Obviously, I couldn't putt it out of the hole, so I chipped—and it went in. Afterward, a guy who'd been watching said, "Why did you put the ball back in that plug mark?" I said, "Because it's the right thing to do. It's the Rules of Golf." If I'd placed the ball outside of that hole, I might have five-putted because sometimes that's how it goes. If you know you're not doing it right, it comes back to haunt you. If you put it behind the tree, you put it there, so you play it! Today's kids need to know, don't cheat. Even if you win, you're going to lose in the long run. I firmly believe in that. And that's why I can sleep at night.

■ ■ ■

While Louise and her fellow LPGA members were getting women's professional golf going in the early 50's, there was another seismic shift happening for a different group of golfers. In 1951, when many states were operating under "Jim Crow" laws and codes, a group of black golfers showed up at the Bobby Jones Golf Course in North Atlanta. Because it was a whites-only club, the group was turned away. That courageous group of young men took issue with the laws of the day and inspired a challenge that eventually became the Holmes v Atlanta lawsuit; which ended up going to the Supreme Court in 1955. The Court ruled in favor of Holmes and thus began the desegregation of public golf courses, not only in Atlanta but nationwide.

Growing up in the South, there was a mindset among some folks that I could never fathom. I was raised to believe that people are people. If you do the right thing and you live your life the right way, who am I to say who's any better, worse, or different than me? Perhaps this mindset became more ingrained in me because, as a woman growing up in that era, there were plenty of things that women weren't allowed to do or were frowned on for doing. I can't abide it when folks treat others badly or differently just based on who they are or where they're from.

Having lived in South Florida for much of my professional life, I was fortunate enough to have a pool at most of the homes I owned. During the 1960's, there was a young black man named Charles who did odd jobs and handy work for me around the house. He had a key to the house so that he and his wife could check on things when I was gone. Once, I was planning to leave for a trip and, while I was gone, Charles was going to do some work for me at the house. I said, "Hey, since you're here anyway, please don't hesitate to bring your family over any time and use the pool as much as you want." It didn't even cross my mind that the invitation might cause a problem. I was just talking to a guy I liked and trusted. I didn't see him the way I found out my neighbors did. My offer turned out to be a big problem for them and they couldn't wait to get in my ear about it when I got home. I just couldn't understand it.

One time in 1956, I walked into the locker room in Deluth, Minnesota, and came across another player, Ann Gregory. I really didn't know her well at the time, but I could tell she was terribly upset. Somebody had said something or mistreated her in some way. She didn't say what had happened and it wasn't my business to ask, but I still tried to comfort her as best I could. She told me, "You know, you're the first white person to ever hug me." I was struck by that and had no doubt that whoever had upset her was a Southerner. I guarantee if I'd found out who it was I would have slapped them upside their head. Ann was a true pioneer. Not just because she helped to forge a path for women in golf, but also because she was the first black woman to play on tour. Ann and I later became friends and would see each other occasionally at tournaments.

I wasn't alone in my disdain for injustice. There were a number of us in the early LPGA days that took a bold stance on behalf of our friend and fellow tour player, Althea Gibson. A remarkable woman, Althea was best known as a professional tennis player. The winner of four grand slam titles, she was the first black athlete of either gender to emerge on the world tennis stage. She later turned to professional golf and joined the LPGA. I recall at least two tournaments, one in Baton Rouge and the other in Oklahoma, where the club hosting the LPGA tournament refused to let Althea in the clubhouse. We told the members in no uncertain terms, "No Althea, no tournament!" They acquiesced and so the event was played. It wasn't like our fledgling tour could afford to be picky, but we were all in it together. The alternative of leaving Althea out was unthinkable.

I don't know what it is, but it just drives me crazy when I see people being treated unfairly. In 2002, I was invited to be a guest at the Women's World Amateur Team Championship in Malaysia. I went with my dear friends Pat and Cartan Clarke. One of my standout memories from that week was meeting the women's team from Iran. They were playing in full traditional clothing, and these women had to play golf in the sweltering 100-degree heat in burkas and with every part of their body covered. One of the girls rolled up her sleeves but the man with them, who was their escort and very clearly in charge, told her to roll them back. One of them actually passed out one day. When the Iranian women were sitting at a nearby table during lunch, I asked Pat, "Do you think it would be out of line if I went over and sat with them and talked to them? Nobody is paying any attention to them." Pat said, "I don't think it would be a problem, but ask Mary Capouch." I found Mary, who was chairman of the USGA Women's Committee at the time, and asked. She replied, "Do whatever you want to do."

So, I went over and sat with them for an hour or so. I found out that one of the women had lived in Boca Raton for about 15 years (her husband's company had moved them there) and she spoke English beautifully. Some of the women spoke a little English and some none at all. I talked to them for a while and learned that there was only one golf course in Iran. They have sand greens and, because of that, these women had never putted on grass. At one point I said, "I may get my head handed to me, but if you're going to have golf in your country, you need to have somebody to advocate for you to be able to wear golf clothes." I wasn't talking about shorts or anything—just more forgiving clothes.

It startled the heck out of everyone including me that I chose to engage so much. But it really bothered me to see them trying to play in that heat in those outfits. I ended up seeing them every day and even ended up teaching them how to hold up their skirts to do a chip and run shot. They were quite excited when they came off the golf course knowing that I cared about how they had done each day. By the end of the week, we really had developed quite a wonderful friendship.

"I am Louise's non-golfing friend," said Nancy Lierle, Louise's longtime friend and neighbor. "We talk about all kinds of things—music, opera, and politics. I've always considered myself to be someone with strong values, and

yet I've learned so much more in that regard from Louise. In a way, she's been my moral compass. They don't make people of her standards much any more. She has achieved so much but is still a beautiful human being—a lesson to all of us that you can be true to yourself and still accomplish your goals. I don't know how many people can have that said about them. From the standpoint of loyalty, friendship, and being a straight arrow, she has to be the gold standard."

And That's That!

RANDOM THOUGHTS ABOUT GOLF

Golf is played against only one opponent—yourself.
Figure out that doing well doesn't depend on others doing badly.
No matter how badly you hit one ball, you can recover on the next.
Of course, you can always screw up the next one too.
Remember, you're the only one keeping your own score.
Golf is a true indication of the way you will lead your life.
I've never found an honest person on the golf course
that acts any other way off the course.
Golf is like a love affair. If you don't take it seriously, it's no fun.
If you do take it seriously, it will break your heart. Believe me.

—Louise Suggs

What's written in these pages doesn't come close to doing justice to the fascinating array of people, places, and experiences that have enriched my life in so many ways. It's difficult to put into words how proud I am that I accomplished more than just tournament titles alone. The LPGA stands as a cornerstone of my career. It is the legacy of a small group of us who believed that it was possible—and, by golly, we made it possible.

I'm grateful to have lived long enough to see how successful the LPGA has become. It's my baby, so to speak, and now it's the most successful women's sports organization in the world. When I think about it, I realize we started a new industry for women. Those of us who got the LPGA going had no concept at the time that we'd end up making multi-millionaires out of some of these young women today.

Sometimes it's disappointing that the kids on tour either don't know or respect what we went through all those years ago so that they could have what they do today. When I hear young players gripe, I just want to smack them. In my day, we were lucky to get free cheese and crackers, let alone a courtesy car and all of the other perks they expect when they show up. I was visiting a tournament in recent years and I walked into the locker room. A player, who didn't recognize me, blurted, "Hey, you can't loiter in here." I shot back, "The hell I can't. If I can't, nobody can."

I've joked many times about the difference in the amounts of prize money from my day compared to now. For the 60 professional tournaments I won, my career prize money added up to less than $200,000. Boy, if that doesn't make you want to throw up! I often like to joke that when I start thinking about how much those wins would mean in today's dollars, I get to about $12 million and I have to quit because it makes me sick! All kidding aside, I do wish to heck I could have won some of the money they play for now.

Karrie Webb, a fellow World Golf Hall of Fame member, met Louise for the first time after Karrie won the 1996 Titleholders tournament as a rookie. "My first lengthy conversation with Louise took place in the media center after I won that tournament," said Webb. "She made a point of letting me know that I had just made more money that day than she had in her entire career! As we all know and love Louise, there was no subtlety. There wasn't much else I could say to that but, 'Thank you'." That moment marked the beginning of an enduring friendship.

Fifteen years later, Karrie won the inaugural LPGA Founders Tournament in Phoenix, an annual event held in honor of the LPGA's Founder Members. Louise was present as a VIP guest and, as Karrie walked onto the 18th green to receive the champion's trophy on live television, Louise swatted her on the butt and announced, "Now don't forget. I taught you everything you know."

Karrie didn't forget it. In March 2014, she won her 41ˢᵗ LPGA title— again at the LPGA Founders tournament. During the TV interview after her win, she looked straight at the camera and said, "Louise, I let you down yesterday. But I beat you by one today." She was referring to the phone call she received from her 90-year-old friend and mentor two nights earlier. Louise had called to tell her to go out and shoot 64 on Saturday and position herself to win. Instead, Karrie shot 63 on Sunday to take the title.

"I honestly can't imagine how hard it was for Louise and the other Founders to start a professional women's sporting organization in 1950. They had to have a love for the game that none of us who have come after can understand. Because of them, I've only ever had to worry about making a living from playing golf. Because the LPGA was already established during our lifetime, we sometimes take for granted what we have and what many women did before us; allowing us to make a very comfortable living playing a sport we love."

When Charlie Mechem was LPGA Commissioner in the 1990's, he was the first to make sure that the LPGA Founders were better acknowledged. I am so grateful to Charlie for that. Since then, under Commissioners Ty Votaw, and now Mike Whan, the LPGA has continued to invite me to various events. In a way, I'm like an old trophy they show off and I really enjoy and appreciate that. Cindy Davis, the president of Nike Golf, and Ty, now a senior executive with the PGA Tour, came up with the idea that the LPGA name the Rolex Rookie of the Year Award after me. I got to know both Cindy and Ty back in the early 1990's when they were just young pups working at the LPGA, and I often joke that they are like my own kids—that I taught them both everything they know. Now, it is such an honor to get to present the trophy every year. In conjunction with presenting the award, the LPGA has had me address the new class of tour rookies. I've told them, "I helped build this thing. And if you mess it up, you've got me to answer to."

When I look back, I really don't know how we got through it all and still managed to play golf. That said, I don't think you'll find one of us still alive today who would say they wouldn't go back and do it all over again. We just knuckled down to do what needed to be done because we believed in it so passionately. The challenge itself was as inspiring to us as the golf. We had no idea through all of those tough times that it would lead to something so great. And it is great. And for that, I couldn't be more proud.

The process of writing this book brought back many wonderful memories. It reminded me of how full and interesting my life has been, thanks to golf. The game has been part of me in a way that's hard to describe. I recall how it felt when I first began hitting balls as a youngster and I discovered that there is nothing sweeter than the feeling of a well-hit golf ball. It's like hitting air. Now, eight decades after that wonderful revelation, I feel so very blessed to have had the opportunity to turn something that I loved and enjoyed into a career—a way of life.

And that's that!

The Remarkable Records

Boldface denotes major championship

1940
Georgia State Championship

1941
Punta Gorda Championship of Champions
Southern Amateur

1942
Punta Gorda Championship of Champions
North & South Women's Championship
Georgia State Championship

1945
Doherty Challenge Cup

1946
Doherty Challenge Cup
International Fourball (with Jean Hopkins)
Pro-Lady Chicago Victory National Championship (with Ben Hogan)
Titleholders Championship
North & South Women's Championship
Western Open
Western Amateur Championship

1947
Southern Amateur
U.S. Women's Amateur Championship
Western Open
Western Amateur Championship

1948
Doherty Challenge Cup
North & South Women's Championship
British Ladies' Amateur Championship
U.S. Curtis Cup Team
Belleair Open (professional)
Madmoiselle Magazine Top 10 Merit Award

1949
Western Open
U.S. Women's Open
All American Open
Muskegon Invitational

1950
Chicago Weathervane
New York Weathervane

1951
Carrollton Open

1952
Jacksonville Open
Tampa Open
Stockton Open
U.S. Women's Open
All American Open
Betty Jameson Open

1953

Tampa Open

Betsy Rawls Open

Phoenix Weathervane (tied with Patty Berg)

San Diego Open

Bakersfield Open

San Francisco Weathervane

Philadelphia Weathervane

144 Hole Weathervane Series

Western Open

Leading LPGA money winner—$19,816

1954

Sea Island Open

Titleholders Championship

Betsy Rawls Open

Carrollton Open

Babe Zaharias Open

1955

Los Angeles Open

Oklahoma City Open

Eastern Open

Triangle Round Robin

St Louis Open

1956

Havana Open

Titleholders Championship

All American Open

1957

LPGA Championship (marked career grand slam)
Heart of America Invitational
Vare Trophy for LPGA Scoring Average

1958
Babe Zaharias Open
Gatlinburg Open
Triangle Round Robin
French Lick Open

1959
St Petersburg Open
Titleholders Championship
Dallas Civitan Open

1960
Dallas Civitan Open
Triangle Round Robin
Youngstown Kitchens Trumball Open
San Antonio Civitan Open
Leading LPGA Money Winner—$16,892

1961
Sea Island Open
Naples Pro-Am
Royal Poinciana Invitational
Golden Circle of Golf Festival
Dallas Civitan Open
Kansas City Open
San Antonio Civitan

1962

St Petersburg Open

1966

First woman in any sport elected to the Georgia Athletic Hall of Fame

1979

Elected by Golf Writers Association of America to World Golf Hall of Fame in Pinehurst.

1989

Inducted to Georgia Golf Hall of Fame

2000

Patty Berg Award
LPGA Commissioner's Award
Rolex Rookie of the Year Award named for Louise Suggs
LPGA Teaching Division Hall of Fame

2007

Bob Jones Award by United States Golf Association
Memorial Tournament Honoree

2008

William D. Richardson Award by Golf Writers Association of America

2009

Gold Tee Award by Metropolitan Golf Writers Association

Other Notable Records

Inducted into the LPGA Hall of Fame in 1951.

Served as President of the LPGA from 1955 to 1957.

Through 2013, had more top-five (14) and top-10 (19) finishes in the U.S. Women's Open than any other player in history. These came from 29 appearances.

Won the 1949 U.S. Women's Open by a record 14 shots from Babe Zaharias. The record still stands today in the women's Open, and has been bettered only by Tiger Woods' 15-shot record in the men's U.S. Open in 2000.

Became the first woman to win same tournament three years straight. 1959, 1960, and 1961 Dallas Civitan Open.

From 1950 to 1960, finished in the top three on the money list every year but one.

CPSIA information can be obtained at www.ICGtesting.com
Printed in the USA
BVOW07*2147270714

360540BV00003B/14/P